Aquatic

Life
of the World

Volume 3
Continental shelf–Fiddler crab

Marshall Cavendish Corporation
99 White Plains Road
Tarrytown, New York 10591–9001

© 2001 Marshall Cavendish Corporation

Library of Congress Cataloging-in-Publication Data
Aquatic life of the world.
     p.   cm.
     Contents: v. 1. Abalone–Barracuda — v. 2. Bass–Conservation — v. 3. Continental shelf–Fiddler crab — v. 4. Fin whale–Hydrothermal vent — v. 5. Iceberg–Manatee and dugong — v. 6. Mangrove–Ocean history — v. 7. Oceanography–Puffin — v. 8. Remora–Sea otter — v. 9. Sea pen–Swordfish — v. 10. Tarpon–Wrasse — v. 11. Index.
     ISBN 0-7614-7170-7 (set) — ISBN 0-7614-7171-5 (v. 1) — ISBN 0-7614-7172-3 (v. 2) — ISBN 0-7614-7173-1 (v. 3) — ISBN 0-7614-7174-X (v. 4) — ISBN 0-7614-7175-8 (v. 5) — ISBN 0-7614-7176-6 (v. 6) — ISBN 0-7614-7177-4 (v. 7) — ISBN 0-7614-7178-2 (v. 8) — ISBN 0-7614-7179-0 (v. 9) — ISBN 0-7614-7180-4 (v. 10) — ISBN 0-7614-7181-2 (index)
     1. Aquatic biology—Juvenile literature. [1. Aquatic biology—Encyclopedias. 2. Marine animals—Encyclopedias. 3. Freshwater animals—Encyclopedias.] I. Marshall Cavendish Corporation.

QH90.16.A78 2000
578.76—dc21
                                                          99-086128

ISBN 0-7614-7170-7 (set)
ISBN 0-7614-7173-1 (volume 3)

Printed in Hong Kong

06 05 04 03 02 01   6 5 4 3 2 1

Brown Partworks
Project editor: Bridget Giles
Subeditors: Amanda Harman, Tim Harris, Tom Jackson, James Kinchen, Jane Scarsbrook, Jens Thomas
Managing editor: Anne O'Daly
Designer: Alison Gardner
Picture researchers: Veneta Bullen, Helen Simm
Illustrator: Christopher Jory
Graphics: Mark Walker
Indexer: Kay Ollerenshaw

Marshall Cavendish Corporation
Editor: Marian Armstrong
Editorial director: Paul Bernabeo

WRITERS
Richard Beatty
Dylan Bright
Jen Green
James Kinchen
Dr. Robbie A. MacDonald
Samantha Rohr

Paul L. Sieswerda
Dr. Sergio Steffani
Dr. Robert Stewart
Dr. Robert Stickney
Dr. Laurence G. Riddle
Brian Ward

PICTURE CREDITS
Bio-Photo Services, Inc.: Kerry Dressler 162, 163, 181, 183 **Bruce Coleman:** Jane Burton 138, 143, 190, Alain Compost 170, Jeff Foott 16, Rinie van Meurs 160, HPH Photography 140, Andrew Purcell 146, Kim Taylor 189, Gunter Ziesler 180 **Corbis:** 185 **Ecoscene:** Sally Morgan 143 **ESA:** 187 **Getty Images:** Stuart Westmorland 154, Keith Wood 133 **Gillette Entomology Slide Collection:** Howard E. Evans, 158, Whitney S. Cranshaw 159, Gregory B. Walker 159 **NASA:** 164, TOPEX/Poseidon Mission for Office of Earth Science, Washington DC-Jet Propulsion Laboratory-California Institute of Technology, Pasadena, CA 174-5 **NHPA:** B. Jones & M. Shimlock 147, Norbert Wu COVER, 148, 150, 156, 172, 173, 179 **NOAA:** *Animals Photo Collection:* Richard B. Mierement 157; *Coastline Photo Collection:* Mary Hollinger 142; *OAR/NURP:* 136, 166, 186 D. Kersting title page, 168, B. Walden 137, National Marine Fisheries Service 155; *National Park Service:* Richard Frer 182; *Reef Photo Collection:* 134, 144, Mohammed Al Momany 135, 176 **Papilio Photographic:** 145, 178 **Science Photo Library:** W. Haxby, Lamont-Doherty, Earth Observatory 133

CONTENTS

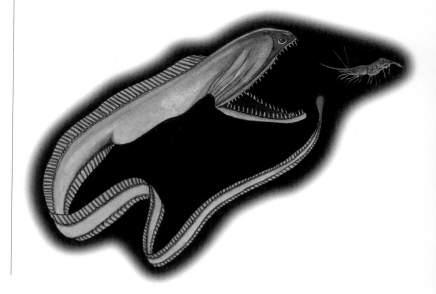

CONTINENTAL SHELF

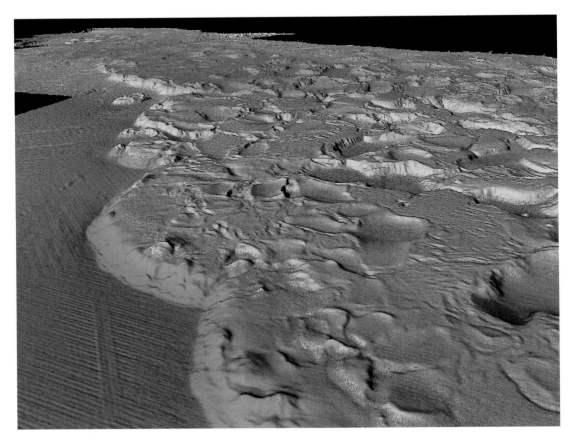

◄ A sonar image of the Gulf of Mexico. The continental shelf (red, yellow, and green area) ends suddenly at the shelf break, where the continental slope (light blue) drops down to the much deeper ocean floor (dark blue).

FACT FILE

Organisms found

Abalones; algae; barnacles; blue whales; clams; cod; crabs; eelgrasses; herrings; humpback whales; jellyfish; kelp; lobsters; mackerel; manatees and dugongs; mussels; plankton; seals; sea otters; sea snails; sea squirts; sea turtles; sea urchins; seaweed; shrimp; sponges; starfish

Human activities

Drilling for oil, minerals, and natural gas; fishing; searching for fossil and archaeological remains

The continental shelves are gently sloping underwater terraces that extend from the coast to a point called the shelf break, where the seabed falls away rapidly as the continental slope. Continental shelves make up around 8 percent of the total area of the oceans and are found all over the world, although their width and depth vary greatly. With rich mineral deposits and fisheries located close to the shore, continental shelves are among the most important areas of the ocean to people.

Many of the world's most productive fisheries are found over continental shelves, where upwellings in ocean currents carry nutrients from the seabed to the surface. The anchovy and sardine fisheries off the west coast of South America and the cod fishery off the northeastern United States are examples of this. Large amounts of oil and natural gas are also extracted from the continental shelves, and deposits of valuable minerals, such as sulfur, are often present. International treaties have been signed that give countries exclusive rights to exploit the resources on the shelves that border their coasts.

SHELF GEOLOGY

Beneath layers of sediments are rocks that form the continental shelves. These tend to be similar to those that form the

WHERE IN THE WORLD

Continental shelf
From the coast down to the shelf break, which is at an average depth of 435 ft (135 m)

SEE ALSO

- Archaeology
- Exploration
- Fishing
- Gulf of Mexico
- Ocean floor
- Oceanography

bordering dry land. Over thousands of years, changes in sea level regularly expose or cover parts of the shelves, and the remains of ancient land features, such as river valleys, can often be found there. At present, sea levels are fairly high, so the submerged portions of the shelves are large, exceeding 240 miles (400 km) wide in places. The average depth of a shelf break is 435 feet (135 m), but in areas such as Antarctica, where the land is weighed down by a thick layer of ice, the shelf break may be 1,200 feet (365 m) deep or more.

Some of the sediments that cover the continental shelves are created by the eroding action of waves pounding against the seashore. Other sediments come from dry land, carried into the sea by rivers. The importance of these two processes varies from coastline to coastline. In areas where there are no large rivers, or where the rivers form large estuaries that trap most of the material they are carrying, sediments on the continental shelf build up slowly. In contrast, places such as the Gulf of Mexico, fed by the Mississippi River, have thick sediment layers. Once they are deposited on the bottom, the sediments are left relatively undisturbed. By studying the depth and composition of shelf sediments, scientists can find out about an area's geology and history.

SHELF HISTORY

Ancient archaeological sites have been found on continental shelves in some areas, such as northwest Florida. There, rising sea levels submerged large areas of dry land around 10,000 years ago. The remains of extinct animals and plants, as well as early human tools and settlements, lie preserved in the sediment. Using sonar, divers, and submersibles, scientists have been able to recover some of this evidence. ◆

▼ Continental shelves are rich in natural resources. This is an oil rig in the North Sea, on the continental shelf off the coast of Great Britain.

CORAL

Corals may look like multicolored plants, or even rocks, but they are actually made up of animals called polyps. Although they often live in large colonies, most polyps are very small—less than ¹⁄₁₀ of an inch (3 mm) in diameter. The coral polyp has a mouth in the center of a ring of tentacles and is similar in shape to its close cousin the sea anemone (uh-NEH-muh-nee). There is a wide variety of coral shapes and structures: some corals are flat and rounded, others are upright and branching, and some even look like the human brain.

STONY CORALS

The polyps that make up stony corals have many tentacles like sea anemones, but they secrete a limestone structure around them for shelter and protection. Because coral polyps do not have an internal skeleton, the limestone they secrete also gives them support, and this allows them to form larger colonies than they would without it (up to several feet in diameter). Groups of stony coral

colonies make up huge reefs such as the Great Barrier Reef off the coast of northeastern Australia. Usually the corals grow on top of the empty skeletons of old corals—so even if the reef is hundreds of feet deep, only a thin surface layer is actually alive.

OCTOCORALS

Another main group of corals is the octocorals, which have just eight tentacles (*oct* means "eight"). These corals are made

▲ These stony corals secrete their limestone skeletons from the lower half and base of the columns.

▲ A large single polyp, with tentacles contracted, of the coral *Fungia scutaria*. Polyps of *Fungia* species can grow up to 10 inches (25 cm) across. Fungia are a type of stony coral that do not form colonies but do live on coral reefs.

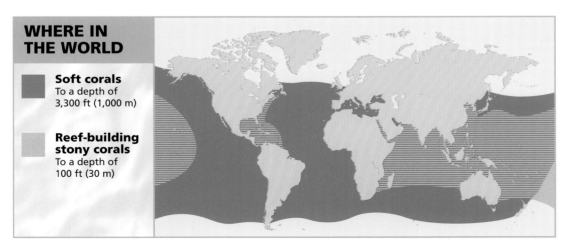

WHERE IN THE WORLD

Soft corals
To a depth of 3,300 ft (1,000 m)

Reef-building stony corals
To a depth of 100 ft (30 m)

up of three smaller groups: the soft corals, the fan corals, and the sea pens and sea feathers. The soft corals, which are particularly common on reefs in the Indian and Pacific Oceans, produce small stonelike particles of limestone instead of producing a complete limestone skeleton.

The fan corals secrete a small amount of limestone, which helps them branch out in a fanlike shape. The sea pens and sea feathers have a similar shape and mode of life to the fan corals, but they live on the seabed and have specialized polyps that pump water into the coral structure to inflate it and help it keep its shape in the absence of a complete limestone skeleton.

FEEDING AND BEING FED

Most corals feed at night by capturing food with their tentacles, which contain stinging cells. When all the polyps of a colony extend their tentacles at the same time, they form a continuous mesh like a fishnet. This can be used to capture and paralyze animals ranging in size from fish to small shrimp. A fold in the stomach wall connects the polyps of a colony to one another; a coral colony therefore has one big group stomach.

All of the reef-building corals also have tiny plantlike organisms called algae living in their stomach wall. The algae and the coral have a mutualistic relationship, (they help each other survive). The algae use sunlight to produce food via a process called photosynthesis, and the coral polyp uses some of this food. In return, the limestone structure of the coral and the stinging cells of the polyp provide protection for the vulnerable algae. ◆

◄ A cross section of a soft coral showing the tentacles arranged around the top, the mouth in the center, and a tube leading down to the gut.

mouth   tentacle

gut

FACT FILE

Name
Reef-building stony corals (Scleractinia)

Habitat
Mostly in water less than 100 ft (30 m) deep and warmer than 64°F (18°C)

Food
Plankton or small fish, depending on size of polyps

Breeding
Sexual reproduction by larvae; asexual reproduction by budding to form coral colonies

Lifespan
Not known for individual polyps

Size
Individual polyps may be from 1/10 in (3 mm) to 12 in (30 cm) wide

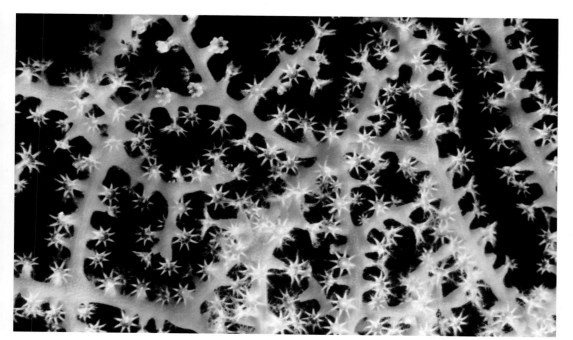

◄ The tiny star-shaped animals visible in this close-up are the polyps that make up the colony. The polyps are joined together by sheets of tissue in this octocoral.

SEE ALSO

- Algae
- Coral reef
- Digestion
- Invertebrate
- Photosynthesis

CORAL REEF

Coral reefs are the largest animal-made structures in the world, and some of the biggest are visible even from space. They consist of mainly the limestone skeletons of reef-building stony corals, but they are also made up of soft corals, sea fans, sponges, and limestone-secreting algae, which create many of the reefs' brilliant colors and diverse shapes. Coral reefs provide homes for a huge variety of sea creatures, which live both in and around it and depend on it for food and shelter. A visitor to a reef would see countless invertebrates—such as clams and starfish—nestling among the corals, and brightly colored fish weaving their way through the underwater "forest."

WARM, SHALLOW WATER

Reef-building coral polyps depend for their survival on algae, which live inside the corals and help them grow and secrete limestone. These algae need light to produce food, however, so coral reefs occur only in shallow water (less than 100 feet, or 30 m, deep), where sunlight

is able to reach them. Below this depth, mostly nonreef-building corals (octo-corals) grow. Reefs are also found mostly in the seas and oceans around the equator and do not develop in waters with a temperature below 64°F (18°C). Coral reefs are made up of layer upon layer of the old, empty limestone skeletons of coral polyps; only the outside layer contains living polyps. When these die, new polyps grow on top, and the reef gets bigger.

▲ **A brightly colored fish nestles among corals in a reef off the coast of North Carolina.**

FACT FILE

Organisms found
Barnacles; bristle worms; butterfly fish; crabs; octopuses; sea cucumbers; sea horses; sea slugs; sea urchins; shrimp; sponges; starfish; wrasse

Threats
Tourism; pollution; coastal development; clams; crown-of-thorns starfish; scallops; parrot fish; surgeonfish

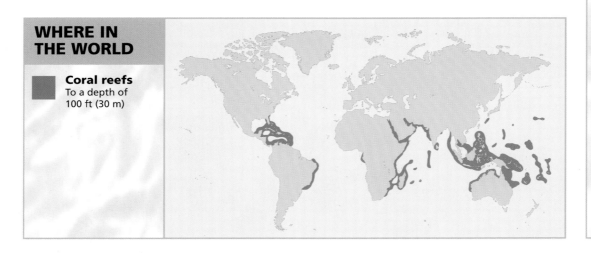

WHERE IN THE WORLD

■ **Coral reefs**
To a depth of 100 ft (30 m)

TYPES OF CORAL REEFS

Coral reefs around the world can be divided into three major types: fringing reefs, barrier reefs, and coral atolls. A fringing reef runs along the coastline and grows slowly outward, away from the land. Barrier reefs are similar to fringing reefs, but there is a deeper lagoon area between the coast and the reef. Atolls are crescent- or ring-shaped reefs surrounding a central lagoon, and they can occur miles from land.

British naturalist Charles Darwin (1809–1882) first suggested how and why the three types of reef were formed in his subsidence theory. He said that atolls might have formed originally from fringing reefs around volcanic islands that sank into the sea. As the islands slowly sank, the corals kept growing upward to form barrier reefs and, finally, atolls. Some coral atolls are over 60 million years old and their bases can be thousands of feet deep.

REEF ZONES

Reefs have four main zones: the reef front (or windward reef), which faces the wind; the reef crest; the reef facing away from the wind (leeward reef); and the reef flat, or lagoon area. The windward reef is battered by waves and has very fast-growing branching corals. Behind this is the reef crest, which is made up of limestone-secreting algae and strong branching corals. Behind this is the leeward reef, which is generally narrower than the windward reef and contains slower-growing corals. Finally, there is the reef flat, where bits of coral broken by wave action are deposited. There, on the more stony surfaces, algae grow, and in softer, sandy areas sea grasses grow. ◆

SEE ALSO
• Algae
• Coral
• Great Barrier Reef
• Island
• Sponge

▼ **Coral reefs support such a wide diversity of aquatic life that they have been likened to tropical rain forests.**

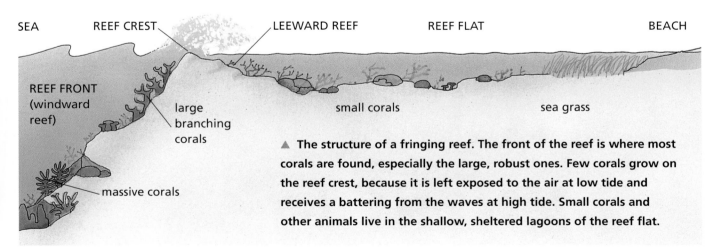

SEA   REEF CREST   LEEWARD REEF   REEF FLAT   BEACH

REEF FRONT (windward reef)

large branching corals

small corals

sea grass

massive corals

▲ **The structure of a fringing reef. The front of the reef is where most corals are found, especially the large, robust ones. Few corals grow on the reef crest, because it is left exposed to the air at low tide and receives a battering from the waves at high tide. Small corals and other animals live in the shallow, sheltered lagoons of the reef flat.**

CRAB

Crabs belong to a group of invertebrates called crustaceans. Like other crustaceans, their bodies are protected by a hard covering called the exoskeleton and divided into three regions: the head, the thorax or midsection, and the abdomen or tail. In crabs, the head and thorax are fused together and covered by a tough shell called the carapace (KAR-uh-paes); the abdomen is reduced in size and folded up beneath the body like a small flap. Female crabs carry masses of eggs beneath this flap-like abdomen, and these eggs hatch into as many as 3 million tiny larvae called zoea, which float among the plankton as they develop.

Like other crustaceans, crabs molt when they need to grow, leaving an empty exoskeleton behind. They must hide from predators to protect their soft body while the new case hardens.

MOVING AROUND

Crabs have five pairs of legs, which are jointed like those of other crustaceans. The front pair is modified into two pincers or claws, which the crabs use for feeding and defense. The other legs are used for walking. Sometimes the last pair of legs are flattened and used for swimming, as in blue crabs. Although

▲ Decorator crabs have tiny spines that snag on to things in the water. Some are also overgrown by algae and sponges. During the day the crab moves slowly or keeps still, hidden by its camouflage.

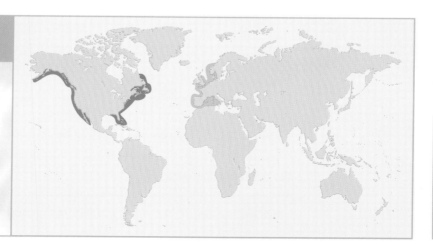

WHERE IN THE WORLD

European edible crab
From tidal zone down to a depth of 330 ft (100 m)

Dungeness crab
From low-tide mark down to depths exceeding 600 ft (180 m)

SEE ALSO

• Crustacean
• Fiddler crab
• Hermit crab
• Spider crab
• Tidal zone

the legs and the pincers provide very effective movement, they are restricted by the way their joints are hinged, and this is why crabs walk sideways.

You can pick up most crabs without getting nipped if you hold them across the widest part of their shell. However, a few particularly aggressive species can reach back and pinch you, sometimes severely. A crab can shed limbs at will to escape an enemy. It does this by contracting a muscle near the base of the limb. The missing leg simply regrows at the crab's next molt.

COMMON CRABS AND HABITATS

The Dungeness crab is a typical member of the group. It has a very broad, reddish shell and powerful pincers. Like most crabs, this species is a scavenger, eating any dead fish or other organisms that it can find, attacking little prey animals such as marine worms, and crushing small mollusks with its pincers. This crab, which is an important food source for humans, lives in eelgrass beds and on muddy or sandy bottoms from shallow waters to depths in excess of 600 feet (180 m). It is found from Alaska down to California. The European edible, or common, crab is very similar to the Dungeness.

The Dungeness crab usually reaches a length of 5½ inches (14 cm) but can grow much larger. The largest of all crabs is the Japanese spider crab. Its rounded body is relatively small at about 18 inches (45 cm) across, but the crab's legs are immensely long, and its pincers can span up to 12 feet (3.7 m).

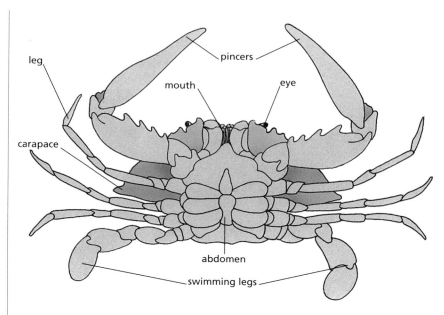

▲ This illustration of a swimming crab shows (from the underneath) the mouth, eyes, abdomen, carapace (shell), pincers, and legs.

Many crabs live in the intertidal zone, spending part of their lives submerged and part exposed to the air. The ghost crab is a common shore crab on sandy tropical beaches, leaving its burrow at night and running swiftly to catch its prey. It can move as fast as 7 ft (2 m) per second. This species lives above the high-water mark and seldom enters the sea, but it burrows down deep into wet sand. A few tropical crabs have left the sea completely, roaming around in moist forest habitats. These land crabs still must return to the sea to breed. Other crabs have adapted to life in freshwater. ◆

◀ Like other crustacean larvae, this hermit crab zoea, less than ¼ inch (0.6 cm) long, will molt several times before it looks like its parents.

FACT FILE

Name
Dungeness crab
(*Cancer magister*)

Habitat
Muddy/sandy shores and eelgrass beds

Food
Dead animals, worms, mollusks, smaller fish

Breeding
Couple pair several days before molting and mate after female molts; the female stores sperm, and eggs are fertilized under female's abdomen; eggs hatch at sea and mature in the plankton

Lifespan
Up to 13 years

Size
Up to 10 in (25 cm) wide

CROCODILE

Crocodiles are large, semiaquatic reptiles that have inhabited Earth since the time of the dinosaurs. These massive predators are found in tropical freshwater and saltwater environments throughout the world. They prefer swamps, marshes, and shallow, slow-moving rivers. There are 21 crocodilians (members of the crocodile family). Present-day crocodilians include 7 species of alligators (this subgroup also contains the closely related caimans); 13 species of true crocodiles; and 1 species called a gavial (or gharial).

Crocodiles are very vocal animals. They communicate by making roars, snorts, and growls, and they also make use of nonvocal communication such as posture, odors, and touching. Males defend their territory from invasion by other crocodiles, although serious injury rarely occurs. In some species, such as saltwater crocodiles, both males and females defend their territory.

CROC PHYSIQUE

Crocodiles and alligators are similar in appearance, but most crocodiles' snouts are thinner compared to the more rounded snout of alligators. In addition, the alligator's lower fourth tooth is not visible when the mouth is closed, as it is in crocodiles. Certain species of crocodiles also grow much larger than alligators, making them the largest reptiles on Earth.

Crocodiles use their strong tail for swimming and defense. The tail can deliver a powerful whip and cause severe injury to the victim. Although

▲ Crocodiles are fierce predators that tackle large prey. This Nile crocodile has dragged a vulture into the water and is tearing up its body. It will swallow each chunk whole.

crocodiles may seem slow, they are capable of short bursts of speed. By pushing with their tail, they can lunge quickly out of the water.

FEEDING

Crocodiles spend most of their time in water, searching for food. Young crocodiles eat small prey such as insects and other invertebrates, while adults feed on fish, birds, and mammals, as well as other reptiles, which they catch in their jaws. Larger prey is taken underwater to be drowned and torn into smaller pieces by the crocodile's rolling and twisting motion. Crocodiles are unable to chew, so they swallow their food whole. Their

FACT FILE

Name
Nile crocodile
(*Crocodylus niloticus*)

Habitat
Rivers and slow-moving, shallow freshwaters

Food
Mammals, fish, birds, reptiles, and amphibians

Breeding
Two months after mating, female lays up to 50 eggs in hole in ground

Lifespan
Possibly 70 to 100 years

Size
Up to 20 ft (6 m) long

throat has a valve that closes to prevent water from entering as they eat.

Nile crocodiles, which are found in the Nile River and throughout much of Africa, grow to an enormous size: up to 20 feet (6 m) long. These huge freshwater predators attack large prey such as zebras, warthogs, wildebeest, humans (although rarely), baby hippopotamuses, and even lions. Prey is attacked while it is drinking or trying to cross the river.

PARENTING SKILLS

Although crocodiles are large, ferocious predators, they are one of the few reptiles that provide parental care for their young. After mating, the female builds a large nest of mud and vegetation, in which she lays her eggs. She deposits about 50 eggs and covers them with soil. The mother will not leave her nest for three months—not even to feed—while the eggs incubate. Many predators such as mongooses, monitor lizards, badgers, hyenas, and humans seek out crocodile eggs.

During hatching, the baby crocodiles call to their mother from inside the nest. The female uncovers the nest and carefully uses her powerful jaws to carry the little crocodiles down to the water. She will guard her babies from predators, including large male crocodiles, for five to six months.

STATUS

Crocodilians worldwide are under constant threat of becoming extinct due to overhunting, poaching, and habitat loss. Conservation programs and laws have been established to protect crocodiles in many areas. Captive breeding programs, wildlife refuges, and law enforcement have helped some crocodile species to survive. ◆

▲ **When swimming underwater, crocodiles hold their legs up close to the underside of their body, making them even more streamlined.
DETAIL: Unlike alligators, crocodiles have a long, thin snout, and the fourth tooth in their lower jaw is visible when their mouth is closed.**

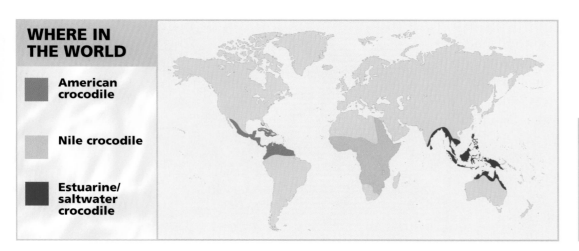

WHERE IN THE WORLD

- American crocodile
- Nile crocodile
- Estuarine/ saltwater crocodile

SEE ALSO

- Alligator
- Endangered species
- Everglades
- Reptile

CRUSTACEAN

Crustaceans are members of an enormous group of animals called arthropods—animals whose body is surrounded and protected by a jointed case called an exoskeleton. Many arthropods, such as insects, spiders, and scorpions, live on land, but most crustaceans live in the sea. There are almost 40,000 different crustaceans known to science, and this number increases every year as new species are discovered. Crustaceans are so common that they have been called the insects of the sea. They are found in almost every type of aquatic environment.

Crustaceans are generally described as aquatic arthropods with gills, jaws, and two pairs of antennae (jointed, movable sense organs). However, some, such as barnacles, vary markedly from this basic body plan.

The most familiar group of crustaceans are the decapods. The members of this group are usually classified into categories such as lobsters, crabs, and shrimp, but these are not scientifically accurate names, and there are many decapods that do not fit easily into any of these categories. True lobsters, for example, have large pincers and are more closely related to freshwater crayfish than they are to other animals that are often called lobsters, such as the clawless spiny lobster. Almost any long slender decapod can be called a shrimp, and some shrimp are not closely related at all. Decapods are only one of 38 crustacean groups; other crustaceans are generally smaller and show a wide variety of body forms.

SUITS OF ARMOR

Crustaceans are invertebrates, or animals without a backbone. Instead of having bones inside their body as vertebrates (animals with a backbone) do, they have a hard exoskeleton that protects them from the outside like a suit of armor. The exoskeleton is jointed, allowing the animal to move around.

▼ Crustaceans live in a variety of habitats. This tower was built by a crayfish from balls of mud. The tower conceals the entrance of the crayfish's home in a freshwater stream.

◄ A Pacific lobster after molting. The empty exoskeleton, or slough, is on the lower right.

FACT FILE

Arthropods
The largest group of invertebrates. Includes insects, crustaceans, and spiders. These animals have jointed legs, exoskeletons, and segmented bodies

Crustaceans
Arthropods that generally live in water and breathe through gills

Exoskeleton
The hard outer covering of an arthropod. They are sometimes called shells

The hard shell cannot expand as the animal grows, so crustaceans shed their shell at regular intervals. A new shell forms beneath the old armor, which is then discarded. The new shell is soft at first, allowing the body to expand, but it hardens after a few days. This process of shedding shells is called molting, and a freshly molted crustacean is very vulnerable to predators until its new shell is hard. Most crustaceans continue to molt and grow throughout their life. The largest crustaceans weigh up to 44 pounds (20 kg) and have few natural enemies other than humans.

BODY PARTS

Crustaceans characteristically have jointed body parts called appendages. The appendages follow the same basic plan but are modified according to their function. Appendages may function as legs, sense organs, breathing organs, or mating organs. Because of the way in which their body and appendages are adapted, crustaceans are able to crawl,

▼ Acorn barnacles attached to a rock. The tiny crustaceans live inside the visible tough shells.

burrow, swim, bore into wood, or live permanently attached to rock.

The bodies of all crustaceans are made up of segments—small sections that are adapted for different uses. In crustaceans such as lobsters and crabs, the segments are fused together to form three main regions: the head, the thorax, and the abdomen. The head and thorax may also be fused together and covered by a solid shield called a carapace (KAR-uh-paes), which protects the internal organs. Many of the segments carry a pair of appendages. The appendages on the first few segments at the front of the body usually form mouthparts. They are used to cut, grind, and handle food passed to the mouth by the legs and pincers. Appendages a little farther back are legs that may be used for walking or swimming.

NERVES AND SENSES

The nervous system of a crustacean is quite different than that of a vertebrate. A crustacean does not have a true brain, and its nerve cord runs along the underside of the body—unlike our spinal cord, which is positioned down our back. Small thickened areas of this nerve cord function as a simple brain.

Very small crustaceans have primitive sight organs called eyespots, which can probably only detect light and dark, but larger species such as lobsters, crabs, and shrimp have highly developed compound eyes. These are made up of groups of smaller light-sensing organs, and they provide excellent vision. Some crustaceans, such as shore crabs, rely on their eyesight to avoid predators such as seabirds. Their compound eyes are often mounted on stalks and can be raised to provide better all-around vision.

The long antennae are important sense organs for all crustaceans. They function as organs of touch and taste. In many cases the antennae are longer than the rest of the body.

BREATHING AND BREEDING

Lobsters, crabs, and most other crustaceans breathe using banks of feathery gills protected beneath the carapace, or shell. To provide a good oxygen supply, water is pumped over the gills by the beating of specially adapted appendages. The blood of crabs and lobsters is very different than that of

▲ **Banded cleaner shrimp are common throughout tropical waters. They get their name for their habit of cleaning parasites and dead tissue from the skin of living fish.**

vertebrate animals like humans. Instead of being iron-based and red, invertebrate blood is copper-based and green.

Many small crustaceans breed by releasing eggs and sperm into the water, where fertilization takes place. However, *Daphnia*, a water flea found in ponds and ditches, broods its young inside its shell until they become miniature versions of the adults. In larger crustaceans, such as shrimp, crabs, and lobsters, the female carries her eggs beneath her abdomen. In this way they are protected from predators. When the larvae (young forms) hatch, they have fewer segments than the adults. As they grow, however, they molt in typical crustacean manner and gradually come to resemble their parents.

Some crustacean larvae float near the surface of the ocean. These transparent creatures usually bear long spines that keep them from sinking and provide some protection from predators. Crustacean larvae form an important part of the plankton, which is a vital food source for many other animals.

HABITATS

Crustaceans can be found in almost all aquatic habitats and at all depths. Some even live in the fluid released from deep-sea hydrothermal vents, which is poisonous to most life-forms. Several types of shrimp live in caves. These shrimp are usually white and lack eyes.

Brine shrimp live only in flooded salt lakes, and when these dry up the shrimp produce eggs that can survive for many years in dry conditions. Larger fairy shrimp live in temporary pools such as rain puddles. Their eggs can resist drying and freezing; they hatch quickly once the rains come. ◆

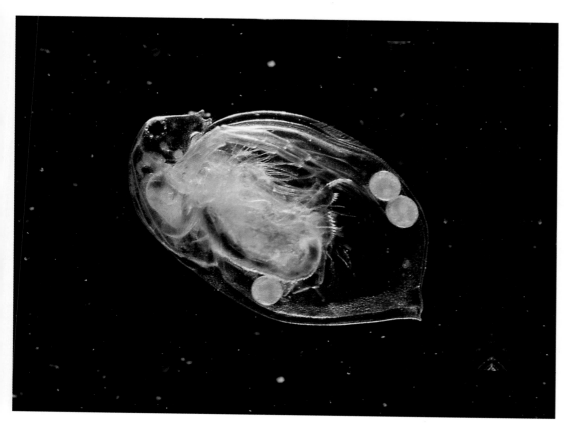

◀ The three eggs inside the transparent shell of this *Daphnia*, or water flea, are clearly visible in this close-up photo.

CUTTLEFISH

Like their relatives the squids and octopuses, cuttlefish belong to the group of complex mollusks called the cephalopods (SEH-fuh-luh-pahds). The common cuttlefish has a head attached to the mantle, which is a muscular structure shaped like a short, flattened cone. Surrounding the mouth are eight short, sturdy tentacles, or arms, that can be moved around and used to direct the body during swimming. The tentacles have sucker cups along their entire length and can be used to grasp and manipulate objects. This cuttlefish also has two longer tentacles with suckers at the large, spoonlike ends. These can be shot out rapidly to catch food items, such as shrimp and crabs. The salivary glands of the common cuttlefish secrete venom that paralyzes their victims, and the cuttlefish's beaklike mouth and rasping tongue tear up the food before it is swallowed.

Cuttlefish vary in size and habitat. The smallest, *Sepia idiosepius*, is less than 1 inch (20 mm) long and lives in rock pools attached to seaweed. Coastal

◄ **Face-to-face with a common cuttlefish. The head bears two huge eyes and eight grasping arms, or tentacles. Cuttlefish also have two sticky tentacles, but these are generally hidden and shot out only for catching their prey.**

species of *Sepia* can reach up to 20 inches (50 cm) long. The ram's horn cuttlefish is widespread in deep waters.

JET PROPULSION

Most of the time cuttlefish maneuver slowly on the seabed, hover above it, or direct themselves by moving a skirtlike fin around the edge of the head and

FACT FILE

Name
Common cuttlefish (*Sepia officinalis*)

Habitat
Coastal waters in Mediterranean, North Sea, and Atlantic Ocean

Food
Invertebrates in surface waters

Breeding
Males develop stripy coloration, and arms become specialized for copulation; females release eggs into water, where they become attached to seaweed; young resemble miniature adults

Lifespan
1–3 years

Size
4–20 in (10–50 cm) long

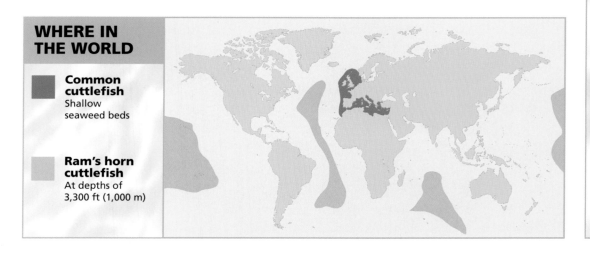

WHERE IN THE WORLD

Common cuttlefish
Shallow seaweed beds

Ram's horn cuttlefish
At depths of 3,300 ft (1,000 m)

mantle in a kind of rippling action. However, when they want to move quickly, these cephalopods can swim using jet propulsion. They draw water in to the space between mantle and body and then expel it quickly through a funnel below the arms and mouth. This causes the animal to move in the opposite direction. The funnel can be pointed in nearly any direction, but the fastest movement is seen when the cuttlefish shoots backward like a torpedo at speeds of up to 25 miles per hour (40 km/h) to escape from danger. When alarmed, cuttlefish can also squirt out a jet of ink to confuse predators.

ADVANCED MOLLUSKS

Like most mollusks, cuttlefish have a shell. Instead of being large and on the outside of the body, however (like that of a snail, for example), a cuttlefish's shell is reduced and on the inside. The shell of the common cuttlefish is shaped like a surfboard and filled with tiny chambers. This cuttlebone, as it is known, is used to control buoyancy (the ability to float). As the amount of fluid and gas alters in the shell's chambers, the cuttlefish either sinks or floats. *Sepia* cuttlebones are often found washed up on coastlines.

COLORFUL CHARACTERS

Like many cephalopods, cuttlefish can change their color by expanding and contracting tiny colored disks in the skin. Especially important is the cuttlefish's ability to blend with the color of its background, but it can also change color depending on behavior and mood. For example, stripes pass along the body during courtship, and the body becomes pure white when the cuttlefish is alarmed. Many species emit light (an ability called bioluminescence). *Sepiola*, for instance, glows in the dark through the actions of light-emitting bacteria that live in pouches in its skin. ◆

▲ The empty chambers in a cuttlebone. When these are not filled with gas, the cuttlefish lies buried in the sand on the seabed; when the chambers are filled with gas, the cuttlefish becomes more buoyant and starts swimming and hunting for food.

◄ This brightly colored animal, which occurs in Sulawesi, Indonesia, is called the flamboyant cuttlefish. Although it is a rare species, it is not endangered.

SEE ALSO

- Biogeography
- Invertebrate
- Mollusk
- Nautilus
- Octopus
- Squid

DEEP-SEA ORGANISM

◄ **This longnose catshark is a member of one of the few shark families found in the ocean depths. Scientists will probably find more of its relatives as they learn more about the deep sea.**

The deep sea contains two main types of organisms: those that swim or float between the surface and the seabed, and those that live on the bottom. There is little light in the deep sea, so green plants and algae, which trap energy from sunlight using the process called photosynthesis, cannot grow there. The absence of these organisms, the vital first link in almost all food chains, means that very little food is produced in the deep ocean. Most nutrients arrive from other habitats.

Some deep-sea animals swim to the surface waters each night to eat the tiny floating organisms of the plankton. Others sieve out and eat the dead material that sinks down from the sunlit zone. These creatures are in turn eaten by a variety of meat-eating animals that also eat each other and almost anything else that moves.

FLASHES OF LIGHT

In the absence of sunlight, many deep-sea organisms produce their own light (a process called bioluminescence) using light organs dotted around their bodies. The flashlight fish has bright light organs and uses them for signaling other flashlight fish and for hunting. Some organisms, such as anglerfish, use light organs like fishing rods, while still others have light organs in their mouths to attract prey. *Malacosteus*, unlike most deep-sea fish, can see red light and uses its red light organs as headlights to illuminate prey. The prey animals cannot see the red light and are unaware that they are being hunted.

Bioluminescence is also important as a form of camouflage. At depths of around 3,300 feet (1,000 m), the small amount of daylight that filters down will silhouette a fish when seen from below. Certain species of deep-sea fish, most notably hatchetfish, are able to sense the color and intensity of the light shining on their backs and emit the same light from their bellies, making themselves invisible from below.

ANIMALS OF THE DEEP

Many types of animals are found in the ocean depths, from octopuses, squids, and fish to corals, sponges, jellyfish, and crabs. It is difficult for scientists to gather information on many species, though, since few living specimens have been observed in their natural habitats.

Because they live in permanent darkness, deep-sea animals generally lack pigments or have only melanin, making them appear black or transparent.

The bodies of deep-sea creatures often take on bizarre shapes because their skeletons and muscular systems are much reduced, and this lowers their density. Because of their food-poor surroundings, some species have evolved massive jaws and teeth that enable them to tackle prey many times their own size. An example of this type of organism is the gulper eel, whose jaws make up 80 percent of its weight.

The deep-sea floor is covered with a layer of sediment partly made up from the bodies of organisms falling from above. Bottom-dwelling creatures such as crabs, mussels, sponges, and corals feed on the falling particles and are in turn eaten by predators such as sharks and rays. These animals have small eyes and poor vision, relying instead on highly sensitive electroreceptors to detect small electrical pulses given off by their prey. They use their sensitive lateral line organs to detect movements in the water. ◆

SEE ALSO

• Anglerfish
• Bioluminescence
• Exploration
• Ocean trench

▼ A gulper eel luring its shrimp prey with its luminous tail end, which emits reddish flashes or glows. These eels have huge jaws with elastic cheeks that can swallow even large prey whole. Scientists have been able to study only dead or damaged examples of this rare fish, so it is not known if this is really how the eel catches its prey.

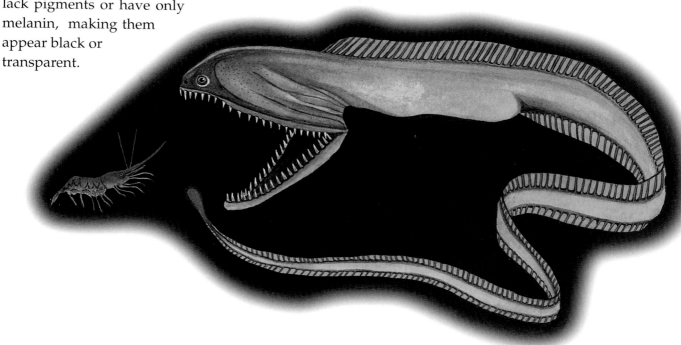

DIGESTION

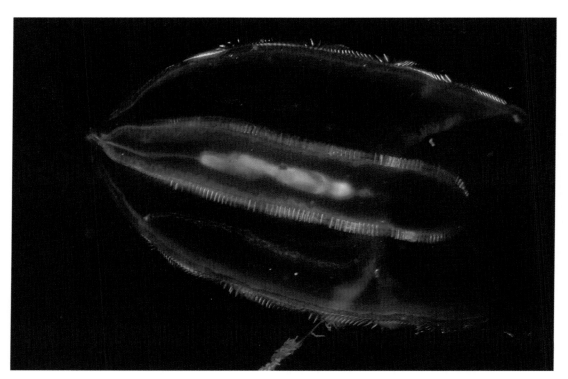

◄ **Inside this transparent comb jelly, a shrimplike animal called krill is being rapidly digested. Comb jellies are marine invertebrates that digest their food internally. Wastes are expelled through the mouth or via microscopic anal pores—tiny holes in the animal's skin.**

All living things need to obtain nutrients from their surroundings to survive. The source of these nutrients varies from creature to creature. Green plants and some microorganisms take in simple substances, such as water and carbon dioxide, and build them into larger molecules, such as sugars, using energy from sunlight. In this way they can make their own "food." The process is called photosynthesis.

Other organisms cannot trap energy in this way. They need nutrients as a source of energy for the chemical reactions inside their cells and to regulate and control these reactions. The nutrients in a creature's food are not always in a form that can be absorbed and used. The process of converting food into usable nutrients is called digestion.

Life processes also produce wastes, which would be fatal if they were allowed to build up inside a creature's body. Excretion is the removal of waste substances from the body.

SIMPLE ORGANISMS

The simplest form of digestion, external digestion, is used by bacteria, tiny single-celled microorganisms that are found almost everywhere. Bacteria convert their food into usable nutrients by releasing molecules called enzymes into their surroundings. There are many different types of enzymes, and each triggers a particular chemical reaction. Those used in the digestive process, called digestive enzymes, usually break down large molecules, such as carbohydrates (sugars and starches), into

FACT FILE

Digestion
The breaking down of food to release simple molecules of usable nutrients such as proteins and sugars

Excretion
The removal of the waste products of digestion and other bodily processes

smaller pieces. The bacterial cell is surrounded by a cell membrane, which large molecules cannot cross. Small molecules, however, readily enter the cell, where they can be used by the bacterium. Bacteria are able to sense the type of food present, then release the appropriate enzyme to break it down. Excretion is equally straightforward: wastes pass out of the cell by crossing the cell membrane.

Amoebas and other protozoans (plantlike and animal-like single-celled and simple organisms) use a different form of digestion, engulfing food items before breaking them down. The food does not cross the cell membrane. Instead, it is drawn into a deep pocket in the membrane. This pocket breaks away from the membrane to form a bubble-shaped enclosure called a vacuole. Enzymes enter the vacuole, break down the food inside, and release nutrients into the cell. The vacuole eventually rejoins the cell membrane, and any undigested contents are expelled.

COMPLEX ORGANISMS

Larger organisms composed of many cells have more complex digestive systems. Perhaps the simplest of these is found in the sponges. Channels run throughout a sponge's body, and water is pushed along these tubes by beating rows of tiny hairlike cilia. Food particles swept along in the current are engulfed and digested by cells lining the channels in the way described above for amoebas. This is an example of cell specialization: some cells provide structural support, others create the current, and only a few play a part in digestion. The nutrients absorbed, however, are distributed to the whole organism.

Jellyfish and sea anemones (uh-NEH-muh-nees) have digestive systems that are more specialized than the sponge's. These creatures have baglike stomachs with a narrow opening at one end. Prey is paralyzed with stinging tentacles and passed through the opening into the stomach. Cells in the walls of the stomach release digestive enzymes, which break down the prey, and absorb the nutrients released. This system is a more efficient way of dealing with large food items than the bacteria's method of digestion because both food and enzymes are trapped in an enclosed space. There, the food can gradually be broken down without valuable nutrients drifting away into the environment and being lost. Unfortunately, enzymes can digest a food item only from the outside, so larger food particles can take a long time to break down. Typical prey for a jellyfish, such as a small fish, can occupy the stomach for hours or even days. Starfish and sea urchins get around this problem by grinding their

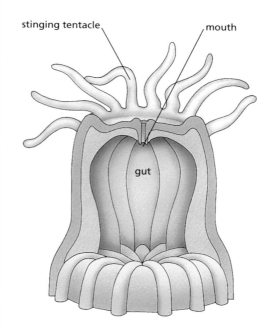

stinging tentacle   mouth

gut

FACT FILE

Extracellular digestion
Food is broken down outside body cells. Invertebrates, vertebrates, and bacteria perform extracellular digestion. Digestion by enzymes in a vertebrate's stomach is one example of this

Intracellular digestion
Food is broken down inside body cells. Protozoans digest food in this way. Some invertebrates perform both types of digestion; hydra, for example, release enzymes onto food and use vacuoles

◄ Corals are carnivorous (meat-eating) invertebrates. They capture prey such as larvae with their stinging tentacles, which then push the meal into the coral's gut through the mouth. Enzymes in the gut digest the prey, and wastes are expelled through the mouth. This is an example of extracellular digestion.

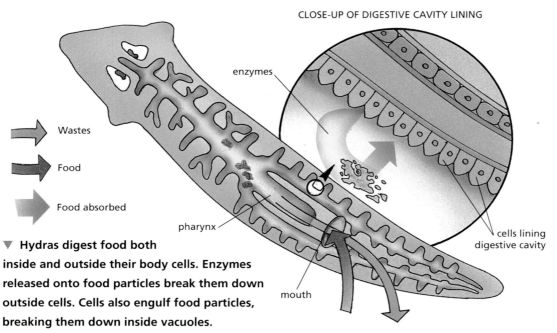

CLOSE-UP OF DIGESTIVE CAVITY LINING

enzymes

Wastes

Food

Food absorbed

pharynx

mouth

cells lining
digestive cavity

◄ **The digestive
system of a
planarian, a flat-
worm. The mouth is
on the underside of
the worm, and the
pharynx can be
extended out of the
mouth like a tube.
Food is broken down
by enzymes, then
absorbed by cells
lining the digestive
cavity. The highly
branched digestive
cavity delivers food
to the entire body.**

▼ **Hydras digest food both**
inside and outside their body cells. Enzymes
released onto food particles break them down
outside cells. Cells also engulf food particles,
breaking them down inside vacuoles.

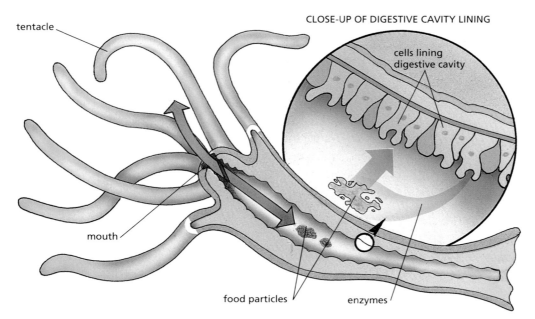

CLOSE-UP OF DIGESTIVE CAVITY LINING

tentacle

cells lining
digestive cavity

mouth

food particles

enzymes

FACT FILE

**Simple saclike
digestive
systems**
The animal has a
baglike digestive
cavity with one
opening for food
to enter and
wastes to exit.
Present in inver-
tebrates such as
corals, sea
anemones, hydra,
jellyfish, and
comb jellies

**Complex tube-
like digestive
systems**
The animal has a
digestive cavity
with an entrance
for food and a
separate exit for
waste material.
Present in most
invertebrates and
all vertebrates

food into small fragments using bony
plates in their mouths before passing it
on to the stomach.

One limitation of all baglike digestive
systems is that the single opening must
function both as a mouth and as an
anus—the point of exit for waste material that cannot be broken down. So,
once the animal has eaten enough to fill
its stomach, it must wait until the meal

has been digested and the wastes
expelled before feeding again. Almost
all other animals avoid this problem by
having a tube-shaped, or linear, digestive system, with a mouth at one end
and an anus at the other. Because food
passes through the tube from one end to
the other, each section can become
specialized for a particular function,
either digestion or excretion.

VERTEBRATE DIGESTION

Digestive specialization is most apparent in vertebrates (animals with backbones), such as fish. Food enters a fish's digestive system through the mouth, where teeth in the jaws and throat grind it into small pieces. From there it passes to the stomach, a large, acid-filled chamber, where it is reduced to the consistency of soup. Beyond the stomach lies the intestine, the longest section of the digestive system, where enzymes go to work on the fish's meal and where the nutrients are absorbed. Finally, the indigestible components of the food are expelled through the anus.

Some fish have an additional section, called a crop, between the mouth and the stomach. The crop is an extendable sac in which food can be stored before passing to the stomach. This organ allows the fish to take in a large quantity of food quickly, then digest it at leisure.

There are many variations on this basic plan, influenced by the fish's diet. Meat is far easier to break down than plant material. Fish that eat meat, such as barracudas, often have pointed teeth that allow them to grip slippery prey, which they swallow whole. They have large, elastic stomachs to accommodate their victims, and their intestines are fairly short. In contrast, plant-eating fish, such as the pacu from the Amazon River, grind their food thoroughly with bony plates in their mouths and have tightly coiled intestines, which would be several times the length of their bodies if stretched out.

Fish dispose of wastes in a number of ways. Some wastes are released into the water via the gills or skin, but most are filtered from the blood by organs called kidneys. The kidneys produce the waste solution urine, which is expelled from the body via the anus. ◆

SEE ALSO

- Bacteria
- Bladderwort
- Cichlid
- Ecology
- Fish
- Food web

▼ The main organs of a typical fish's digestive system. The various parts appear differently in different fish. Some fish have small mouth openings, for example, and suck prey in. Others have large mouths, which they use to grasp their prey.

teeth

mouth

stomach

intestines

anus

DOLPHIN

Dolphins are appealing, intelligent sea creatures, well known for their love of play and friendliness to humans. A school of dolphins leaping in the waves is a popular sight. Despite their appearance, dolphins are not fish but mammals: air-breathing, warm-blooded animals whose young feed on their mother's milk.

Dolphins are members of several families of small- to moderate-sized toothed whales. The family of true, or oceangoing, dolphins contains about 35 species; the five species of river dolphin belong to three other families. Dolphins are similar to porpoises, but whereas dolphins generally (but not always) have beak-shaped snouts and pointed teeth, porpoises are generally smaller and have rounded snouts and spade- or chisel-shaped teeth. Until quite recently, and particularly in the United States, the term *porpoise* was used for any small, toothed whale. Most scientists now agree, however, that the six species

of porpoises belong to a different family from dolphins. Killer whales and pilot whales are members of the oceangoing dolphin family, but because of their larger size, they are normally referred to as whales rather than dolphins.

Dolphins are found in seas and oceans worldwide, except the coldest polar waters. Many dolphins live in shallow coastal waters, while others inhabit the open oceans. River dolphins live in freshwater and are found in large rivers such as the Amazon in South America and the Ganges in India.

SIZE, SHAPE, AND MOVEMENT

All dolphins share a similar body shape, but they vary considerably in size. The smallest species, Heaviside's dolphin, reaches only

FACT FILE

Name
Common dolphin (*Delphinus delphis*)

Habitat
Warmer temperate and tropical waters

Food
Squid and small fish, including herring, sardines, and mackerel

Breeding
Once every 2–3 years, with a gestation period of 10–12 months. Live young are suckled for 5–6 months

Lifespan
25–40 years

Size
On average between 6½ and 8 ft (2 and 2.5 m) long, and weighing up to 240 lbs (75 kg)

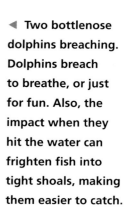

◀ Two bottlenose dolphins breaching. Dolphins breach to breathe, or just for fun. Also, the impact when they hit the water can frighten fish into tight shoals, making them easier to catch.

4 feet (1.2 m) long. Bottlenose dolphins, a familiar sight in sea parks, measure up to 13 feet (4 m) long and weigh up to 650 pounds (300 kg). The blunt-nosed Risso's dolphin reaches a similar length but weighs up to 1,100 pounds (500 kg). Body colors and patterns vary too. Some species, such as the bottlenose dolphin, are mainly gray, but the hourglass dolphin has distinctive black-and-white markings, and the backs of spotted dolphins are mottled.

Dolphins' bodies are sleek and streamlined. Like all whales, their tails end in wide, horizontal lobes called flukes that beat up and down to propel the animal forward. The curving dorsal fin helps with balance. The two chest fins, or flippers, help the animal to steer, make sudden turns, and brake quickly. The dolphin's tough, rubbery skin feels velvety to touch. Beneath the skin, a thick layer of fat called blubber keeps the dolphin warm in cold water.

Dolphins are expert swimmers, and the fastest species can reach speeds of about 25 miles per hour (40 km/h). Dolphins are able to dive deep in search of food, and they can remain submerged for up to 15 minutes. Mainly, however, they prefer to swim and hunt in surface waters, coming up once or twice a minute to breathe. The single nostril, or blowhole, on top of a dolphin's head allows it to breathe without lifting its head up out of the water. But when swimming along, dolphins often prefer to leap right out of the water, so they can breathe without having to slow down. They may leap as high as 20 feet (6 m) in the air and sometimes seem to do so just for fun, though they may also leap to warn other dolphins of danger. This action is known as breaching.

▲ A school of spotted dolphins assuming vertical positions. Dolphins are social creatures that often live in groups. Species that live in open seas can form groups of more than 100 members. Coastal dolphins tend to form much smaller groups.

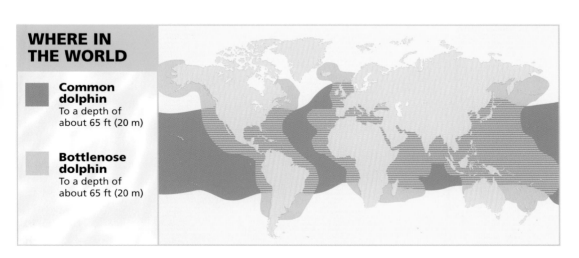

WHERE IN THE WORLD

Common dolphin
To a depth of about 65 ft (20 m)

Bottlenose dolphin
To a depth of about 65 ft (20 m)

SENSES AND FEEDING

A dolphin's small eyes provide good vision but their sight can sometimes be limited by the amount of light in the water. All of the dolphin's body is sensitive to touch, particularly the head. Dolphins make a wide range of sounds, including chirps, squeaks, clicks, groans, and whistles. Many of these noises are too high-pitched for humans to hear. Dolphins use sound to communicate with other group members. Each animal has a unique signature whistle that it uses to identify itself to others. The dolphin's ability to make sounds, coupled with its keen hearing, is used to locate food and to compile a "sound map" of its surroundings.

Dolphins are efficient hunters. They feed mainly on small fish such as herrings and sardines but also on larger

▶ **A dolphin's melon is a fatty organ that focuses the high-frequency sounds the animal produces to locate objects, including prey, in its environment.**

transmitted sound

melon

returning echo

fish, shrimp, and squids. They use their own built-in sonar system to find food, a process called echolocation. As the dolphin swims along, it emits a stream of clicks and whistles. Scientists believe that these noises are focused into a beam of sound by a fatty lump of tissue

▼ **Dolphins use echolocation to locate prey. When hunting, they can work together to herd fish into shoals.**

called the melon at the front of the head. The sound waves spread out through the water, and when they meet an object, such as a fish, they bounce back. From the returning echoes, the dolphin can tell the size of its prey and the direction in which it is moving. Once the prey animal has been located, the dolphin moves in, seizes it, and swallows it whole.

WAYS OF LIFE

River dolphins and some porpoises lead solitary lives. Most dolphins are social animals, however, living in a group known as a school or pod. These schools usually contain less than 20 dolphins but can hold more than 100 members. Members of the school often cooperate when hunting. Dolphins will also help an injured member of their group. They support the wounded animal with their bodies, keeping it afloat so that it can breathe.

Many dolphins mate in spring and early summer. A single calf is born, tail-first, 10 to 12 months later. Other females might assist the mother at birth and help the calf to the surface so that it can take its first breath. The young dolphin is well developed and can swim immediately. It suckles its mother's milk, often for more than a year.

DOLPHINS AND HUMANS

Since ancient times there has been a strong bond between humans and dolphins. Some dolphins seem to seek out human company and are often found riding the bow waves of ships. Some of these creatures, known as friendlies, arrive daily in coastal areas to swim and play alongside humans. There are many stories of dolphins

▲ Dolphins are protected by law in the United States. As this sign shows, penalties for willfully harming them are severe. In many waters, however, dolphins are still in danger of being killed by tuna fishers, and some South American species are used as crab bait.

rescuing injured or stricken swimmers. On parts of the African coast, dolphins are known to help local fishers net their catch. Tests in public aquariums show that dolphins learn new skills quickly and can pass on newly acquired abilities to other dolphins.

However, humans are not always friendly toward dolphins. In Japan and China, dolphins are hunted for their meat. In parts of the Pacific, dolphins often swim with shoals of tuna. As the dolphins leap out of the water, they guide fishers to the tuna shoals, and the dolphins get trapped in the nets set for the fish. In the last 30 years roughly 6 million dolphins have died this way. In the United States and some other countries, dolphins are now protected by laws that demand that fishing boats use nets with panels that dolphins can see and leap over. Elsewhere, dolphin hunting still continues. ◆

FACT FILE

Name
Bottlenose dolphin (*Tursiops truncatus*)

Habitat
Tropical and temperate waters, coasts and open seas

Food
Larvae, small fish, squid, and shrimp

Breeding
Calf born after 12-month gestation; nursed for up to 18 months

Lifespan
25–40 years

Size
3–13 ft (1–4 m) long and up to 1,400 lbs (650 kg)

SEE ALSO

- Killer whale
- Mammal
- River dolphin
- Whale

DRAGONFLY

Large, colorful, and aerobatic, drag-onflies are familiar insects to many people. The group includes both true dragonflies and damselflies. There are about 5,500 dragonfly and damselfly species worldwide, including around 650 in North America. Dragonflies hold their wings out stiffly when resting, while damselflies fold their wings over their backs like butterflies. This can be used to distinguish dragonflies from damselflies.

CARNIVOROUS NYMPHS

The young dragonflies, called nymphs, are usually green or brown and live underwater. The nymph stage generally lasts for less than one year, although several species can spend two or three years or even longer as nymphs. Some dragonfly nymphs live in streams, while others prefer still water. They live on the bottom mud or among weeds and eat a variety of freshwater creatures, including small fish. Some species rely on eyesight to find prey, others on touch and vibration. They seize their victims with an extendable lower lip. Equipped with sharp hooks to grip prey, this struc-ture can be extended out from beneath the head very quickly.

Damselfly nymphs breathe by using three bladelike gills at the end of their bodies. A dragonfly nymph, however, pumps water in and out of its abdomen, at the rear of the body, and over the gills located in a chamber inside. A strong pulse of the gill chamber sends a jet of water out of the abdomen, shooting the nymph away from danger.

▲ A colorful dragonfly at rest on a stalk. The bright colors indicate that this male is ready to mate.

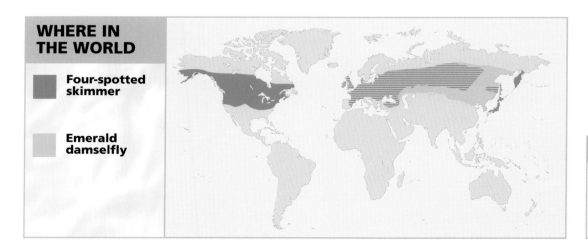

WHERE IN THE WORLD

■ Four-spotted skimmer

■ Emerald damselfly

SEE ALSO

• Insect
• Invertebrate
• Lake and pond
• Reproduction

▶ Dragonfly and damselfly nymphs have extendable bottom lips that cover the lower part of the nymph's head when not in use. The extendable lip has two hooks at the end for grabbing prey.

Dragonfly nymphs molt (shed their skin) several times during their development. Before the final molt, the nymphs of most species climb up the stalks of water plants into the air, where they emerge as adults from the cast skin.

AEROBATIC ADULTS

Adult dragonflies live for a few weeks or months. They catch insects that are in flight or swoop down to pick them off the ground. Dragonflies are helped by their huge eyes and by their speed and maneuverability on the wing. Like a helicopter, they can fly sideways and even backward, changing direction almost instantly. Although most individuals stay close to the place where they emerged, some use their flying skills to seek out new habitats.

A few species, such as the four-spotted skimmer, sometimes migrate in large swarms for hundreds of miles. Males of some species are territorial, defending stretches of rivers or ponds against rivals.

Before mating, a male dragonfly seizes the female by the head or neck with claspers at the end of his body. Mating then takes place either in the air or on vegetation. After mating, the male might keep hold of the female or stand guard near her until the eggs are laid. In some species, the female lays eggs by dipping the end of her body into the water while still flying. In others, she clambers beneath the surface to place the eggs on submerged plant stems.

Like other freshwater creatures, dragonflies are vulnerable to pollution and habitat destruction, and several countries have organizations devoted to their conservation and study. Sometimes artificial environments compensate for the loss of dragonflies' natural homes. In South Africa, for example, farm reservoirs have become important dragonfly habitats. A pool suitable for dragonflies has clear water and plenty of stems for the nymphs to climb before emerging as adults. ◆

▲ The nymphs of dragonflies (left) and damselflies look very different.

FACT FILE

Name
Four-spotted skimmer (*Libellula quadrimaculata*)

Distinctive features
Four wings with two spots on each

Habitat
Variety of stagnant waters, from lowlands to high altitudes

Food
Insect larvae and other insects

Breeding
Mate while in flight; female lays eggs by lowering tip of abdomen into water

Lifespan
2–3 years (mainly as larvae)

Size
Larva: 1 in (3 cm) long; adult: up to 2 in (5 cm) long

◀ A damselfly rests on a leaf.

DUCK

FACT FILE

Name
Common eider (*Somateria mollissima*)

Habitat
Arctic and subarctic coasts; migrates south in winter to Atlantic coasts

Food
Crabs, mollusks, shrimp. Feeds by diving more than 30 ft (10 m) underwater and prying shellfish off rocks

Breeding
Mate in spring/ summer; 4–6 pale green eggs laid, which hatch after one month

Lifespan
From 4 to 5 years

Size
Up to 23 in (58 cm) long; wingspan up to 25 in (63 cm)

Ducks are waterbirds that are related to geese and swans. They are found in wetlands, rivers, lakes, and oceans. Ducks are generally smaller than swans and geese, with a shorter neck and a broader beak. Most ducks are 14 to 26 inches (36 to 66 cm) long and weigh 2 to 4½ pounds (0.9 to 2 kg). They are generally capable fliers, but they are best suited to life on water. They have a broad body and webbed feet that act like paddles for pushing them along. Their legs are set well back on the body, which makes them graceful when afloat but awkward on land, where they walk with a waddle.

Ducks have a thick coat of feathers to keep them warm in cold water. At least once a year, birds molt (shed) their feathers and grow a new set. Unlike most other birds, ducks lose all their long wing feathers at once, so for a brief period of time they cannot fly at all.

Male ducks have bright feathers for most of the year but dull plumage while molting, so they can hide from predators at their most vulnerable stage.

DIVING DUCKS AND DABBLERS

There are around 90 species of wild ducks. They can be divided into two main groups: dabbling ducks and diving ducks. Dabblers such as mallards and teals feed at or just below the water surface. With their broad, flat bill they sieve plants and small creatures from the water. Diving ducks, on the other hand, swim down below the surface to feed on plants, fish, crabs, snails, clams, and other aquatic creatures. Some can stay submerged for half a minute or more.

Diving ducks are found both in freshwater wetlands and in saltwater. Freshwater divers include pochards, tufted ducks, and goldeneyes. When diving below the surface, these birds swim with their feet, keeping their wings tight against their body. Marine diving ducks include eiders, scoters, and mergansers. Scoters are strong swimmers that spend most of their time at sea. Mergansers are fish-eaters. Their long, narrow bill has jagged edges for keeping a tight grip on slippery fish.

Some eiders breed in Norway and Iceland, inside the Arctic Circle. The female eider plucks her soft breast feathers to line her nest. These warm, wispy feathers, called eiderdown, are also used by people to insulate quilts and comforters.

WAYS OF LIFE

Ducks find their mates in winter. The males, called drakes, display their bright feathers to win a partner. In spring some species travel (migrate) to safe breeding grounds, often in cooler climates. The female builds her nest in reeds or grasses, in a tree hole, or sometimes in a burrow, and lays between 6 and 12 eggs. Her dull plumage helps her to hide as she incubates the eggs. The chicks hatch in less than a month: they are well developed, with open eyes and fluffy feathers. Soon after hatching,

they are able to swim and feed themselves. The chicks stay close to their mother and follow her wherever she goes. In five to eight weeks they learn to fly. In the fall many ducks gather to migrate to winter feeding grounds, which are in warmer places where the water does not freeze over. Some species fly only a short distance on migration or do not migrate at all; others cover thousands of miles. ◆

▲ A red-breasted merganser dives after its prey.

◄ The serrated (sawlike) bill of the merganser duck prevents its victims from escaping before the bird has had time to swallow.

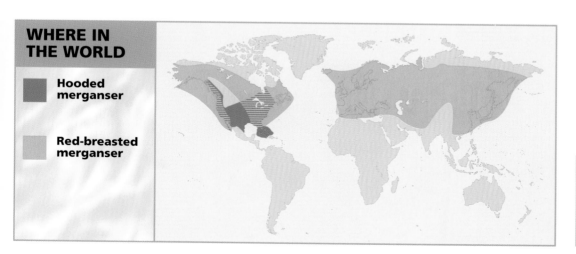

WHERE IN THE WORLD

Hooded merganser

Red-breasted merganser

SEE ALSO

• Bird
• Lake and pond
• Vertebrate

DUCKWEED

◀ **Some duckweeds are extremely small. Here the fronds of *Lemna valdiviana*, sometimes called duckmeat, are shown with a grain of rice, revealing just how tiny they are.**

uckweeds are small aquatic plants that float on, or just beneath, the water surface in quiet streams and calm pools. They are the smallest and simplest of the flowering plants (angiosperms). They are not divided into stems, roots, and leaves like most flowering plants but are made up of small, free-floating oval-shaped structures called fronds, with roots attached directly to their base. These fronds contain one or more gas-filled chambers called aerenchyma (ar-ENG-kuh-muh; see diagram on page 163). *Spirodela* species have the largest fronds, up to ⅘ inch (20 mm) across, while *Wolffia* species are just ²⁄₂₅ inch (2 mm) or less in diameter. *Lemna* species are somewhere between these two, with a frond diameter of ⅛ to ³⁄₁₀ inch (6 to 8 mm).

There are 38 known species of duckweeds worldwide, found mainly in

WHERE IN THE WORLD

■ ***Lemna* species**
Surface waters

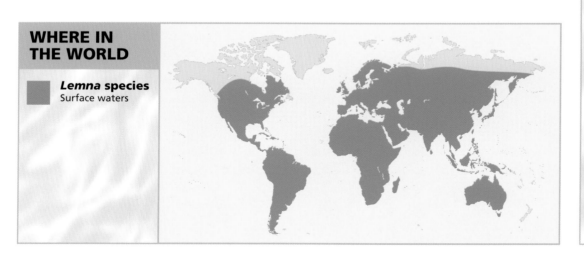

temperate and tropical regions. The duckweed family is particularly well represented in western North America, where nearly half the world's species are present.

MAKING NEW PLANTS

Duckweeds reproduce both sexually and asexually. Sexual reproduction is carried out during the summer when each duckweed flowers and is pollinated (fertilized) by other duckweed plants. The flowers of most duckweed species are very small and are rarely seen. Duckweeds also reproduce asexually by budding off copies of themselves called clones. It is likely that a small Indian duckweed species called *Wolffia microscopia* could reproduce by asexual budding every 30 hours if growth conditions were ideal. In this situation, after around 4 months there would be 1 nonillion (1 with 30 zeros) clones. This would be enough to cover the entire surface of Earth. Fortunately, growth conditions never stay ideal for long, and the duckweed is constantly grazed by fish and other animals in the water, keeping its levels down.

USEFUL DUCKWEED

The explosive growth rate of duckweeds makes these tiny plants useful for cleaning up waters that have been polluted by nutrients from farm fertilizers. This is because the duckweed grows so quickly that it uses up large quantities of the nutrients.

Duckweed is also a very good source of food, since over 40 percent of its dry mass is protein, similar to the amount in soybeans. The plants can therefore be scooped off the surface of the water and fed to farm animals. In addition to

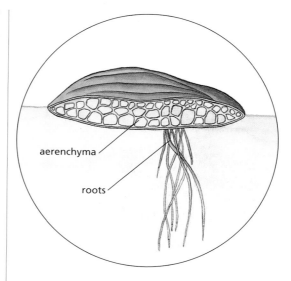

aerenchyma

roots

◄ **A cross section of a duckweed frond, showing the trailing roots and the hollow chambers called aerenchyma. The aerenchyma are filled with gas and give the plant buoyancy, allowing it to float on the surface of the water.**

protein, duckweed also has high concentrations of important minerals.

Many species of freshwater fish eat duckweed to supplement the protein in their diet. These include the grass carp, the channel catfish, the common carp, the goldfish, and some of the important commercial species of tilapia. Ducks, turtles, and crustaceans such as water shrimp, crayfish, and water fleas also graze duckweed. One duckweed species (*Wolffia globosa*), known locally as khainam, is a delicacy eaten by the people of Southeast Asia. ◆

SEE ALSO

- Photosynthesis
- Pondweed
- Water hyacinth
- Water lily

▼ **A close-up of mud midget, or bog mat. This duckweed is found in sluggish waters, often with other duckweed species.**

ECOLOGY

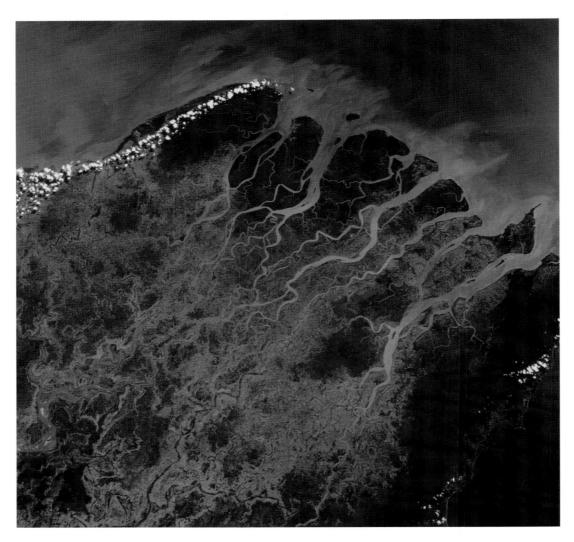

◀ The mouth of the Irrawaddy River, Myanmar (Burma). Like other estuaries, it is an important ecological site. The deep red areas in this infrared photo are healthy rain forests and large mangrove swamps. The plumes of light blue leaving the river's many inlets show the flow of nutrient-rich sediments into the Andaman Sea. This biologically rich delta region was built up from deposits of fertile mud and sand over the last 2 million years.

Ecology is a science based on the study of the interactions between organisms and their environment. Ecologists investigate the abundance and distribution of animals and plants and relate this to the physical and biological characteristics of their environment. In recent years ecology has come to focus in particular on the impact of humans on their environment. As a result, *ecology* has been used as a label for many conservation activities, ranging from domestic recycling to campaigns for saving the whale. Ecology is a broad-ranging scientific discipline, however, that is similar to more traditional sciences such as biology and chemistry.

Ecologists often study more than one species and expand their studies to whole systems and communities that include a wide range of organisms. These large units are called ecosystems because of the complicated web of inter-

FACT FILE

Definition
Ecology is the complex network of relationships between living organisms and particular environments. Ecology is also the study of these relationships

actions between organisms themselves and between organisms and their environment. Similarly, ecology often focuses on studying processes, such as the flow of energy and nutrients and the competition between species for food, rather than the basic biology of an animal or plant. Therefore, while aquatic and land ecosystems differ greatly in their appearance and in the makeup of life within them, many of the processes studied by ecologists are the same on land as in water.

ENERGY FLOW

Life depends on the availability of energy, and the way in which organisms receive energy is the most fundamental of ecological processes. At or near the surface of lakes and oceans, sunlight can be used by plants and algae to make energy directly by photosynthesis. This is an example of primary production. Many other organisms rely on primary producers such as sea grasses, marsh grasses, seaweeds, and single-celled algae to provide them with energy in the form of food.

In aquatic communities primary production is often supplemented by secondary sources of energy from outside the ecosystem. For example, in rivers, lakes, and coastal areas, water running off the land often brings with it dissolved nutrients and silt that is rich in organic matter and energy. The importance of secondary supplies of energy from the land is highest in streams and rivers and lowest in the open ocean, where primary production by plankton provides almost all of the energy entering the system. Some of the world's most productive aquatic ecosystems are the communities that are

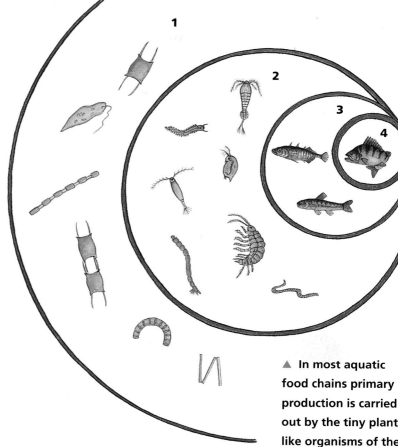

closest to the land, such as estuaries and mangroves, which have primary productivity from photosynthesis as well as high secondary inputs of nutrients from the land.

In addition to primary production by plantlike plankton (phytoplankton), certain marine ecosystems receive a regular input of extra energy from upwelling of cold, nutrient-rich waters from the seabed. Major upwellings occur in the Arctic and Antarctic Oceans as well as along the Pacific coast of South America. These upwellings promote the productivity of plankton and fish, so they attract a range of predators such as seabirds and whales to feed. In some cases, however, the winds and ocean currents that cause

▲ In most aquatic food chains primary production is carried out by the tiny plant-like organisms of the plankton: the phytoplankton (1). These so-called producers are eaten by the tiny animals (2) found in the plankton: the zooplankton. These are in turn eaten by small meat-eating fish (3). Larger predators, such as perch (4), eat the smaller fish. At each stage in the chain, the number of organisms is smaller than that in the stage before. Several linked food chains make up a food web.

upwellings can reverse direction. This has the effect of removing the extra input of nutrients and devastating the structure of the ecosystem.

In coastal areas of Peru and Ecuador, reversal of the coastal upwelling happens every two to ten years and is known as El Niño. The disappearance of nutrient supplements from the deep sea removes the main source of energy for marine communities and causes a failure of the sardine fisheries that support the local economy. Events such as El Niño influence not only local ecosystems but have serious consequences for weather and agriculture throughout the world.

PRODUCTIVITY AND CHANGE

The productivity of ecosystems can be measured in biomass: the total mass or number of living organisms in a certain area. While aquatic ecosystems can be highly productive, many are

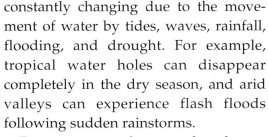

constantly changing due to the movement of water by tides, waves, rainfall, flooding, and drought. For example, tropical water holes can disappear completely in the dry season, and arid valleys can experience flash floods following sudden rainstorms.

Ecosystems such as rocky shores, estuaries, and coastal wetlands are in a constant state of bombardment by waves; they dry up when exposed at low tide but are flooded at high tide, and fresh rainwater and salty seawater are equally likely to flow over them. In many ways, these systems are among the most physically demanding on Earth, and yet biological diversity is rarely as great as when seen in a kelp forest, mangrove swamp, or rock pool. Part of the reason for this diversity is the very breadth of natural conditions and the fact that species with a wide range of adaptations can find a foothold, even a brief one, in these environments.

NICHES

An organism's niche, or the place it occupies in an ecosystem, is defined by factors such as what it eats, what preys on it, its habitat, and whether it is day or night active (diurnal or nocturnal). Organisms that at first seem to be in direct competition can actually coexist in the same ecosystem if they occupy different niches. For example, two barnacle species, *Balanus* and

◀ **An ecologist builds an artificial reef. Corals and other organisms such as algae, moss animals, and sponges will colonize the building blocks. The artificial reef's growth and development will be closely monitored over following years, providing invaluable data on the ecology of coral reefs.**

◀ **A sea otter in kelp. Sea otters are vital to maintaining the biological diversity of kelp forests.**

FACT FILE

Biomass
The total mass or number of organisms in a particular area. Biomass can be an indicator of the productivity of an area

Niche
The place, or role, an organism occupies in an ecosystem. It can be defined by what the organism eats, what preys on it, its habitat, and at what times it is active

Keystone species
Organisms that are vital to the overall health of an ecosystem

Chthalamus, occupy the same shoreline and use the same food resources. Ecologists have shown that on the lower shore, *Balanus* is a superior competitor to *Chthalamus* and can actually smother young *Chthalamus* larvae (young forms). In contrast, on the upper shore, *Chthalamus* survives well because of its greater ability to resist drying out during low tides. The two species occupy slightly different, but overlapping, niches on the shoreline, and competition between them controls their distribution where they overlap.

KEYSTONE SPECIES

The role of predation (who eats whom) in controlling the structure of ecosystems has been emphasized by studies of sea otters living in kelp forests. Sea otters eat a wide range of marine invertebrates such as abalone and sea urchins. These invertebrates are in turn important grazers on the kelp and can limit kelp growth. When otters are removed from an ecological community, for example when they were hunted to extinction in parts of California, the web of interactions between predator, prey, and kelp (a producer) is disturbed. Populations of urchins increase and cause the destruction of kelp beds. Sea otters act as a so-called keystone species, improving the diversity of the whole kelp forest. Removing the keystone reduces the diversity of the ecosystem. When kelp beds are deforested, however, simply restoring the sea otter to those areas is not always possible. This problem shows how important it is to understand ecology and emphasizes the need for conservation measures for endangered species before extinction changes the ecosystem forever. ◆

SEE ALSO

- Biogeography
- Conservation
- Endangered species
- El Niño and La Niña
- Estuary
- Food web
- Kelp forest
- Mangrove
- Wetland

EEL

◄ A spotted moray eel lurks among the corals and sponges on a reef, lying in wait for victims such as small fish.

Eels are long, slender fish, with a long, waving fin running in a continuous line along the length of their back and around under their tail. There are more than 500 species of eels living in the major oceans, freshwater lakes, and rivers around the world. These belong to about 20 different families, the best known of which are the American and European eels (actually found in waters of almost every continent), the American and European conger eels, and the moray eels (all found on the rocky beds of temperate and tropical seas). The South American freshwater electric eel belongs to a group of fish

FACT FILE

Name
American eel (*Anguilla rostrata*)

Distinctive features
103–111 vertebrae, compared to 110–119 in the European eel

Habitat
Lake and river-beds until adult; oceans during spawning and larval stage

Food
Small crustaceans, worms, insects

Breeding
Takes place in Sargasso Sea but details of how the eels mate or spawn are not yet known

Lifespan
Around 15 years

Size
Adult females up to 47 in (1.2 m) long and 15 lb (7 kg) in weight

WHERE IN THE WORLD

Spiny eel
Deep sea

European eel
Lake and river beds

American eel
Lake and river beds

Sargasso Sea

that are different from other eels and known for their capacity to generate a powerful electric discharge. Spiny eels belong to a family of marine eels that are mostly found in moderately deep to very deep waters.

Moray eels are the most widespread of all the eels. These sometimes brightly colored fish have a large mouth and long, sharp teeth and can become vicious if disturbed by divers. Generally they grow to up to 3 feet (1 m) long, but some may even reach 10 feet (3 m) in length. American and European conger eels are strictly marine and can grow to up to 20 feet (6 m) long and weigh more than 110 pounds (50 kg).

American and European eels spawn at sea but grow and mature in freshwater. These eels occupy a variety of habitats—from oceans through estuaries, rivers, and lakes—during their lives. These eels and conger eels spawn in the Sargasso Sea, a free-floating mass of sargassum in the Atlantic Ocean.

A LONG JOURNEY

After several days on the bottom of the Sargasso Sea, the larvae (young forms) of European eels hatch from their eggs. Each larva carries a tiny drop of oil, which allows it to float toward the surface of the water and drift with the Gulf Stream that travels across the Atlantic Ocean. It takes around three years before they reach western European coasts and become elvers, measuring less than 2 inches (5 cm) in length. The elvers migrate up the rivers, crossing all kinds of natural challenges to get into creeks,

lakes, and reservoirs. Once in freshwater, the fish begin to turn yellow. During this time they feed on small crustaceans, worms, and insects, and they grow to 24 to 31 inches (61 to 79 cm) long within 10 to 14 years. Toward the fall, some yellow eels develop a blackish back and a metallic silvery sheen on their sides, and they begin the long journey of 4,350 miles (7,000 km) back to the Sargasso Sea for breeding. Once in the sea, both males and females die after mating and egg laying, and then the cycle begins all over again. Scientists do not yet know why the eels make this journey or how exactly they mate. ◆

▲ A colony of garden eels (also called sand eels). These fish get their name from their habit of planting their tail in the sand with mucus (thick, slimy fluid) and waving in the water with their mouth open, feeding on microscopic organisms.

▲ Like other moray eels, dragon morays have a large mouth with sharp, backward-pointing teeth that prevent slippery prey from escaping. Dragon morays also have large sensory projections on their snouts.

SEE ALSO

• Atlantic Ocean
• Electric fish
• Fish
• Locomotion
• Migration
• Ocean current

EELGRASS

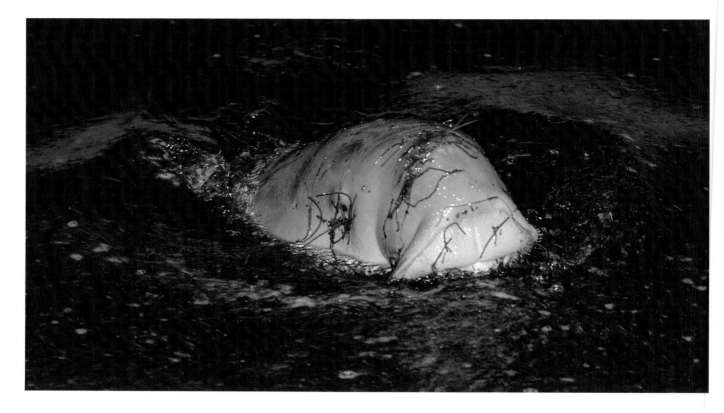

Also known as a sea grass or wrack, eelgrass has long, narrow leaves and is one of the few types of flowering plants (angiosperms) that has a fully marine life. It is related to the familiar grasses we see on land and has a similar structure made up of leaves, roots, stems, and reproductive organs. Like land grasses, eelgrass uses sunlight to make its food in the process called photosynthesis. For this reason, it grows only in fairly shallow water in which sufficient light can penetrate—this depends on the clarity of the water but can be as deep as 100 feet (30 m).

Eelgrasses grow from a horizontal underground stem called a rhizome. The side branches from this are the visible leaf structures that grow up from the seabed and measure ⅓–⅖ inch (0.5–1 cm) wide and up to 3 feet (1 m) long. The rhizome also has roots, which are used mostly for anchorage. The roots of eelgrasses help to hold the seabed together and reduce its erosion.

COMMON GRASSES

Worldwide there are 52 different species of eelgrasses, but one of the best known is *Zostera marina*. Each eelgrass plant reproduces by flowering in the summer and pollinating (fertilizing) other eelgrasses underwater. Shoots bearing ripe, fertilized seeds break off from the grasses and drift in the ocean currents. The ripe seeds eventually sink to the bottom, and if the conditions are favorable, new grasses will grow. *Zostera*

▲ **Like green plants on land, eelgrasses form the basis of food webs in the ocean. Many animals, such as this dugong (a sea cow), feed on their juicy stems and leaves.**

SEE ALSO

- Aquatic plant
- Ecology
- Food web
- Manatee and dugong
- Photosynthesis

underwent a population collapse in the 1930s due to a wasting disease. The population has, however, slowly recovered and recolonized most of the areas in which it was formerly abundant.

GRASSY MEADOWS

Eelgrasses are highly productive plants, and meadows of eelgrass form the basis of many complex underwater communities. These plants are generally found rooted in soft sediments such as sand and mud within the shelter of bays and lagoons. Tropical eelgrass meadows are grazed heavily by fish, turtles, sea urchins, and dugongs. Swans and brant geese are the only animals known to eat the grasses in temperate regions, but fish such as leatherjackets and blackfish graze algae and other small organisms that grow on the surface of the grass.

As well as providing food, the leaves of eelgrasses also protect young fish and invertebrates, including shrimp and crabs, from predators such as larger fish. They also reduce the speed of water currents, which causes particles of suspended food to fall to the seabed. These are caught and collected by a variety of invertebrates such as sea cucumbers and sandworms.

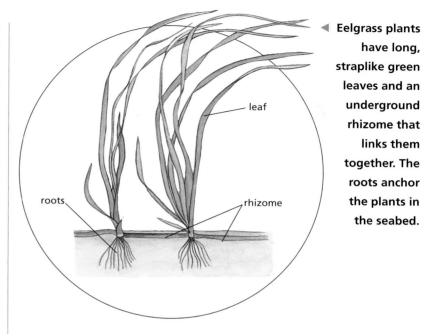

leaf

roots

rhizome

◀ Eelgrass plants have long, straplike green leaves and an underground rhizome that links them together. The roots anchor the plants in the seabed.

HUMAN USES FOR EELGRASS

A species of eelgrass called neptune grass is often found on Mediterranean beaches in the form of sea balls. These are balls of dead, brown eelgrass that have been knotted and rolled up by the action of waves. Large volumes of sea balls are often washed up on seashores around the world. Sometimes people collect the dried grass and use it as packaging or fertilizer. Eelgrasses are also used to treat a number of illnesses, and occasionally fishers eat their sweet-tasting roots. ◆

FACT FILE

Name
Eelgrass
(*Zostera marina*)

Habitat
Along the coast in sandy or muddy sheltered areas and coves

Food
Uses nutrients and sunlight to make own food

Reproduction
Underwater pollination and dispersal in the plankton

Lifespan
Not known

Size
Leaves ⅕–⅖ in (0.5–1 cm) wide and up to 3 ft (1 m) long

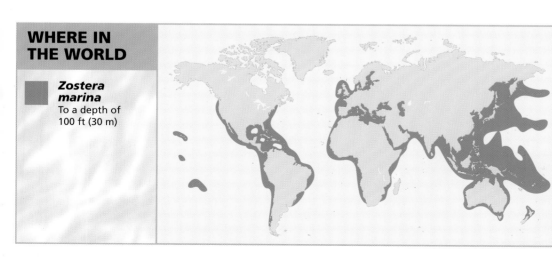

WHERE IN THE WORLD

Zostera marina
To a depth of 100 ft (30 m)

ELECTRIC FISH

Some fish have the amazing ability to use electricity to help them navigate in poor light, to protect themselves, or to stun their prey. This capacity is found in no other group of vertebrates (animals with backbones). There are more than 300 fish species, many unrelated, that have electric organs. The most common of these are the electric rays, which are widely distributed in tropical and temperate seas; the freshwater electric catfish and elephant-snout fish of Africa; the freshwater electric eels and knifefish from Central and South America; and some marine stargazers, which live in tropical and temperate seas and estuaries.

The electric organs of these fish are very different in form and position in the body, but they all have a similar microscopic structure. Each organ looks just like an electric battery. It is made up of many regularly arranged disk-shaped cells (called electroplates) embedded in gel (to keep the electricity from dispersing inside the body) and bound together by connective tissue into a long

tube. Electric rays have an electric organ on each side of the head, but electric eels have three arranged along each side of the body, making up almost half the fish's body weight. In electric catfish, the electric organs are more diffuse, covering the whole body. In marine stargazers, however, they are very small and situated behind the upward-pointing eyes.

▲ **Electric eels can generate both weak electric currents and short shocks of more than 500 volts.**

electric organs

pector

▲ **The internal position of electric organs in an electric ray. The ray springs on its prey, wraps it in its disklike pectoral fins, then stuns the prey with an electric shock.**

WHERE IN THE WORLD

Electric ray
Mostly bottom living: from 30 ft down to 500 ft (10 m to 150 m)

Electric catfish
On the bottom of rivers and lakes

Electric eel
On the bottom of rivers and lakes

Some electric fish can generate extremely powerful electric discharges: up to 220 volts in the electric ray; 370–550 volts in the electric eel, which also generates a much lower continual pulse; and 350–450 volts in the electric catfish. The ancient Romans used the electricity produced by electric rays to cure some health problems in people—an early form of electroshock therapy. Elephant-snout fish and knifefish generate a very feeble electric discharge, usually less than a volt. This discharge is continuous or pulses intermittently.

WHY BE ELECTRIC?

Strongly electric fish use their electric charges for hunting—stunning small fish before eating them—or to protect themselves against their enemies. Weakly electric fish, on the other hand, use theirs to produce an electric field all around their body. Any object or animal that enters the electric field distorts it and is soon detected by receptors on the body's surface.

This system allows the fish to navigate at night and in murky rivers. The electric field can also be used to communicate with other fish of the same species.

MIXED SIGNALS

In each species of electric fish, the electroreceptors are "tuned" so that they pick up only the electric pulses emitted by the fish's electric organ and filter out other electrical noise in the environment. A problem can arise, however, when interference occurs from electricity emitted by nearby members of the same species. Some fish have receptors that detect interference and change the frequency of the electric discharge, allowing fish of the same species to operate in the same area. This is similar to several radio stations in the same city operating on different frequencies; listeners can tune in to only one frequency at a time. ◆

◀ **This Pacific electric ray is a slow-moving species that often lies partly buried in sand or mud, concealed from its prey. It is widely distributed along the Pacific coast of North America. It can generate electric shocks of up to 120 volts, which it uses both to stun prey and to defend itself against any animals that threaten it.**

FACT FILE

Name
Torpedo ray or electric ray (*Torpedo nobiliana*)

Distinctive features
Produces strong electric shocks of between 170 and 220 volts, enough to throw an adult human to the ground

Habitat
Bottom-living on mud and sand of coastal regions in temperate, mostly Atlantic, marine regions

Food
Large variety of bottom-living fishes

Breeding
Bears live young offshore, measuring about 10 in (25 cm) long

Lifespan
Not known

Size
Up to 6 ft (180 cm) and 110 lb (50 kg)

SEE ALSO

- Catfish
- Eel
- Fish
- Hammerhead shark
- Shark
- Stingray

EL NIÑO AND LA NIÑA

El Niño (el-NEE- nyoe) and La Niña (la-NEE-nya) are changes in the ocean–atmosphere, or water–air, system in the tropical Pacific that affect weather around the globe. The tropics lie between the tropic of Cancer (23.5°N) and the tropic of Capricorn (23.5°S). The tropical parts of the Pacific are home to a giant heat engine that drives the winds that blow over Earth.

Normally, sunlight shining on the Pacific Ocean warms the top layer of water. Winds and ocean currents carry the warm water west to form a giant warm pool, about 82°F (28°C), near Indonesia and Australia. The top layer of water continues to heat up, and some water evaporates (turns into water vapor) into the atmosphere. This evaporation transfers heat energy from the ocean to the atmosphere. The air above the Pacific is hot and humid, and great thunderstorms form. During these thunderstorms, many inches of rain fall—some tropical areas get up to 200 inches (5 m) of rain a year. The remaining atmospheric heat drives the winds that blow over Earth.

◄► These three images of the Pacific Ocean were created from data collected by a joint U.S.–French satellite. The colors indicate the temperature of the ocean. The heat of the world's oceans is important since it affects the air above, cooling or heating it and disrupting weather patterns. LEFT: The large red-and-white area is the warm pool of water associated with El Niño. It is spreading all the way from South America up to Alaska, bringing with it heavy rains. RIGHT: Purple and blue areas are the cold pool of water associated with La Niña, which brings drought to North and South America. FAR RIGHT: The pool of cool water has all but disappeared. The ocean has returned to near normal conditions (green).

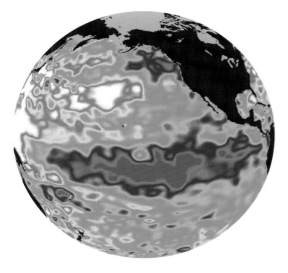

FACT FILE

El Niño
Triggered by the weakening or reversal of westward trade winds. This allows the large mass of warm water normally near Australia and Indonesia to move east to the Americas. Since the water is warmer than normal, more of it evaporates (turns into gas), and this in turn increases rainfall

La Niña
The reverse of El Niño: stronger than normal trade winds move warm water from the central Pacific to the western Pacific. This warm water increases the evaporation rate, which means more rain in Southeast Asia and Australia

LA NIÑA

This giant heat engine does not always run smoothly. Every few years, weather over the Pacific Ocean changes. Some years, trade winds blow strongly from South America to Asia. The winds push the warm water along the equator to the warm pool near Asia. As a result, much more rain than normal falls near Indonesia and Australia. This state of the Pacific is called La Niña.

The strong La Niña winds cause cold water to come to the surface along the equator near South America. This water wells up from the cooler, nutrient-rich layers of water that are underneath the warm layer. The nutrients in this water are good for tiny plantlike algae (phytoplankton). Phytoplankton form the base of the aquatic food chain. Zooplankton (tiny animals) feed on the phytoplankton. In turn, many fish (the most common in this area is the anchovy) and birds feed on the zooplankton.

EL NIÑO

After one to three years of La Niña conditions, trade winds weaken. At that time, warm water near Asia is able to spread eastward along the equator toward South America. At the same time, the wind-driven upwelling that supplies cold water to the eastern Pacific slows. As a result, water near South America warms up by 4–9°F (2–5°C). This warm, nutrient-poor water cannot sustain phytoplankton, and the entire food chain collapses. The anchovies spread out and move away. Seabirds that eat the anchovies starve and many die, and South American fisheries suffer. A few months later, warm water spreads up the coast of North America, sometimes as far as Alaska. At the same time, heavy rains move away from Indonesia toward the east Pacific. The rain moves to the central Pacific near the Gilbert Islands at 180°E. This state of the Pacific is called El Niño.

GLOBAL EFFECTS

During El Niño eastern parts of North and South America get heavy rains, and Indonesia and Australia get less rain or even drought. During La Niña the conditions are the opposite. Indonesia and Australia get heavy rains, and the Americas get drought. ◆

ENDANGERED SPECIES

Although extinctions occur without human intervention, people are a very destructive species, and human activities have a dramatic impact on a wide range of other organisms. The growth of human populations has spelled disaster for many wildlife species in both land and water habitats. Since 1620 more than 500 plants and animals have become extinct in the United States alone, and many other species are on the brink of extinction.

While extinction is forever, endangered species can be saved by a variety of conservation measures. These include protection of particular species or habitats, breeding in captivity, and programs to reintroduce species in areas where they have already disappeared. The Endangered Species Act provides protection for a wide range of aquatic species, and responsibility for saving these organisms from extinction lies with the Fish & Wildlife Service and the National Marine Fisheries Service. In 1999, 69 fish, 9 amphibians, 7 aquatic reptiles, 11 marine mammals, and 1 waterbird, as well as many aquatic invertebrates and plants, were endangered in the United States. The problems faced by these species have several causes, including hunting, habitat loss, and pollution.

A RANGE OF THREATS

Some species, such as sea turtles, are endangered because of a whole range of human activities. Green turtles were once widely caught for food, and their eggs were considered a delicacy. Hawksbill turtles were caught for their attractive shells. Today, commercial

◀ A sea turtle lurks in a crevice of a protected coral reef in the Red Sea. All seven species of sea turtles are endangered. Populations of these marine reptiles have been decimated by hunting, habitat loss, and commercial fishing activities.

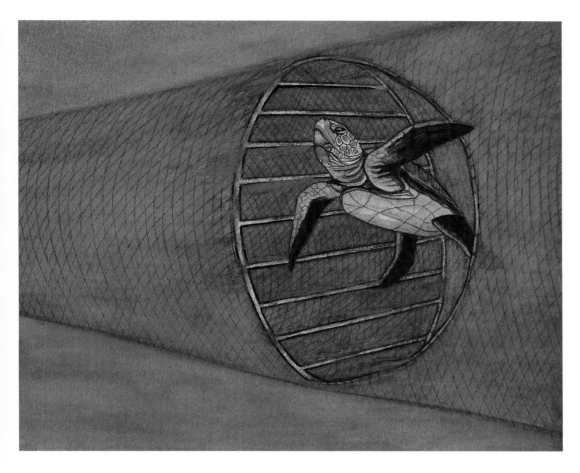

◄ **A sea turtle escapes a shrimp net using a turtle excluder device (TED). TEDs are metal grilles with openings wide enough to let shrimp but not turtles through. The TED leads the turtle to a hole in the net covered by a flap.**

FACT FILE

Name
Green turtle (*Chelonia mydas*)

Habitat
Mostly tropical but also warm temperate oceans

Food
Sea grasses (adults); shellfish and small fish (hatchlings)

Breeding
Breeding season spring/summer; females dig flasklike holes in sandy beaches and lay 3–5 clutches of between 30 and 100 eggs in one season. Eggs hatch after 40 to 70 days

Lifespan
More than 30 years

Size
Up to 4.5 ft (140 cm) long across the top of shell

hunting of turtles is prohibited. However, hundreds are still killed accidentally when they are caught and drowned by fishing nets and lines.

Although they spend their lives at sea, female turtles must return to land to lay their eggs. There, they suffer from habitat loss because nesting sites have been destroyed by beachfront development. Adult females are also disturbed by leisure activities on the shore, and hatchling turtles can get lost on beaches because artificial lighting directs them away from the sea.

Even simple measures can help conserve turtles, however. By adding Turtle Excluder Devices to shrimp nets (required by law in the United States), accidental deaths can be dramatically reduced without affecting catches.

Reducing artificial lighting and stopping off-road driving on beaches during the nesting season can also greatly improve breeding success.

Florida manatees are another example of how human activities can unwittingly place aquatic species on the critical list. Only 1,900 of these large herbivores survive in Florida, with another 100 in Puerto Rico. Besides the dangers of habitat loss, manatees are threatened by human leisure activities. Powerboaters motoring through the Florida Everglades and along the coastline can cause terrible injuries to the manatees by slicing into the slow-moving animals' backs with their propellers. These wounds often prove fatal, and up to one-quarter of all manatee deaths are caused by clashes

◄ In the 1970s there were fewer than 60 gavials in India. Active conservation has led to an increase, but the gavial is still endangered. The creation of sanctuaries and the collection of eggs for hatching in incubators have helped halt the gavial's decline.

with speedboats. Refuges where power-boating is strictly controlled or banned are now in place, and boaters who break speed limits can face severe fines.

OVERHUNTING

Another member of the manatee family that once lived on the coastline of the northern Pacific is Steller's sea cow, which was first described by German naturalist Georg Steller in 1742. The then newly discovered Alaskan coastline provided a rich source of sea otter furs for Russian trappers and fur traders. The trappers needed food to support their hunting expeditions, and the large and docile sea cow was an easy target. By 1768 the last Steller's sea cow was killed by hunters, despite attempts by some Russian naturalists to protect the species. In the tragic history of human impact on the wildlife of North America, this is probably the most dramatic case, with a large and fascinating marine mammal being driven to extinction in only 26 years.

Numerous other aquatic animals have been endangered by overhunting, including the gavial. Like other members of the crocodile family, the gavial was once widely hunted for its leathery skin. It is now illegal to trade in the skin of most wild crocodilians.

HABITAT LOSS

Even aquatic plants may be endangered by human activities. The much-admired western lily is a wetland species that is now restricted to 31 sites spread across southern Oregon and northern California. There are now only 2,000 to 3,000 individual plants left, and these are threatened mainly by habitat loss. Unlike animals, which are generally more capable of moving to new suitable habitats when their homes are threatened, aquatic plants are often the first victims of habitat changes. In the case of the western lily, humans have drained bogs and wetlands to get land for development—in particular, for roads and cranberry farms.

Similarly, pondberry (or southern spicebush), a rare wetland shrub that lives on only 22 sites in southeastern and central United States, is threatened by habitat loss due to wetland drainage, as well as by damage caused by

FACT FILE

Name
Gavial, or gharial (*Gavialis gangeticus*)

Distinctive features
Long, thin snout, which cuts through water easily when swiping at fish

Habitat
Rivers and lakes in temperate regions of South Asia

Food
Mostly fish

Breeding
Often mate on bottom of river; eggs laid after 2 months in hole in ground and hatch after 3 months

Lifespan
85–100 years

Size
Up to 21 ft (6.5 m) long

domestic and wild animals such as hogs. In comparison to aquatic animals—especially mammals such as manatees and whales—plants receive little conservation attention. So, while pondberry bushes do receive some protection in North Carolina and Missouri, there is no state protection in the six other states in which pondberry occurs. Simple measures such as erecting fences to prevent damage by hogs could be enough to prevent extinction of this endangered species. Only large-scale protection of habitats, however, can improve the status of most sensitive aquatic species.

FLAGSHIP SPECIES

Some endangered species are seen as flagships for conservation. One such case is the bald eagle, which is the national symbol of the United States. This species lives mainly on fish and is strongly linked to marine and fresh-water habitats. During the 1950s and 1960s, poisonous chemicals such as DDT ran off farmland into lakes, where they were absorbed into the muscles of fish swimming in the polluted waters. When eaten by the eagles, the chemicals in the fish caused the birds' eggshells to

become so thin that adult birds crushed their own eggs when they were incubating them. An outright ban on DDT usage combined with the promotion of captive breeding and reintroduction programs have brought this bird back from the brink of extinction. Although there were only 450 breeding pairs in the lower 48 states in the 1960s, populations have now increased tenfold—to number more than 4,500 pairs. ◆

▲ Conservationists have found it hard to attract attention to the plight of endangered fish. Exotic species such as this leafy sea dragon inspire concern more easily than less appealing fish do.

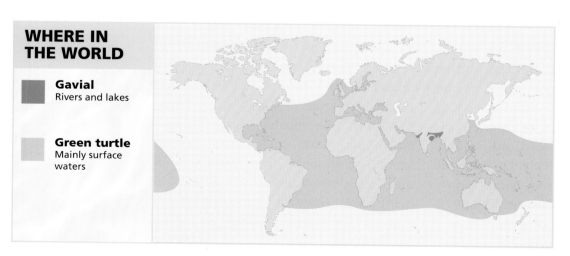

WHERE IN THE WORLD

Gavial
Rivers and lakes

Green turtle
Mainly surface waters

SEE ALSO

- Blue whale
- Coelacanth
- Conservation
- Crocodile
- Leatherback turtle
- Manatee and dugong
- Marine iguana
- Sea otter
- Sea turtle

ESTUARY

A large group of beluga whales in a river estuary in Canada. The whales gather here in summer to give birth to their young away from predators such as killer whales and to feed on shoals of migrating salmon.

FACT FILE

Definition
A place where the tide meets a river current

Organisms found
Those that can tolerate varying proportions of freshwater and saltwater, including fiddler crabs, mangroves, eelgrasses, and mudskippers. Eels and salmon migrate through estuaries on their way between rivers and the sea. Estuaries are also safe nursery areas for the young of many species of marine fish

Threats
Coastal development pollution from cities, shipping, farmland, and industry

An estuary is a water passage where the tide meets a river current. Estuaries are located along coastlines and, in most cases, are places where the salinity (the total amount of dissolved salt in a sample of seawater) is reduced because freshwater is continuously mixing with the saltwater of the ocean. Exceptions to this occur where the amount of water evaporating (turning into a gas) and entering the air is greater than the amount of freshwater entering the estuary. As water evaporates, the salts become concentrated and salinity goes up. Places where this happens are called negative estuaries. More typical estuaries—where freshwater inflow is greater than the rate of evaporation— are called positive estuaries.

HOSTILE ENVIRONMENTS

Conditions in estuaries are constantly changing. Salinity in any place within an estuary will rise and fall as currents carry saltwater upstream during flood tides and as more freshwater enters the estuary during ebb tides. The amount of rainfall, volume of water in the river, and evaporation rate will also affect salinity. Plants and animals that are unable to move around may be exposed to a wide range of salinities each day. Estuaries also receive nutrients and pollutants that enter their feeder streams. Pollutants from hundreds of miles away can build up in estuaries. In many cases, estuaries are environments that can be tolerated only by highly adaptable species.

NURSERY AREAS

Despite the harsh conditions, life flourishes in estuaries. Salt marshes, mangroves, and sea grasses are often found in estuaries. Many animals, including some that support large commercial fisheries, spend at least part of their lives in estuaries. Among these are marine shrimp, some crabs, and numerous fish species. Many of these animals start their lives as eggs released into the water in offshore areas. Currents carry the eggs and newly hatched animals into estuaries, where they find food and grow. As they approach adulthood, they may migrate offshore once again. The dependence of young marine animals on estuaries has led scientists to give the estuarine environment the label "nursery area."

PASSING THROUGH

Some animals move through estuaries as they migrate from one aquatic environment to another. Often, their passage through estuaries is associated with reproduction. Salmon, for example, spawn (lay eggs) in freshwater rivers or lakes, and the juveniles migrate through estuaries to the ocean where they live until they return to freshwater to reproduce. Eels show the opposite pattern: they spawn in the ocean and the young migrate to freshwater, where they grow to adulthood.

HUMAN IMPACTS

Estuaries provide safe harbors for ships as well as access to inland areas. There is also freshwater available in the rivers that feed estuaries. As a result, many important cities and seaports are associated with large river estuaries. Pollutants from factories, chemical plants, oil refineries, sewage-treatment plants, and various other places have caused significant harm to estuaries around the world. Some countries, including many in Europe and North America, now have strict environmental regulations in order to maintain the health and beauty of their estuaries. ◆

SEE ALSO
- Ecology
- Mangrove swamp
- Migration
- Pollution
- River and stream

◀ Sedges growing at the shallow margins of an estuary. Banks of vegetation like this play an important part in cleaning up polluted estuaries. By slowing down the flow of water, they allow pollutants to settle out and become trapped in the sediment. They also absorb lots of water, lessening the impact of flooding.

EVERGLADES

The Everglades is a large, subtropical marsh covering about 4,000 square miles (10,000 square km) of southern Florida. The climate is mild and the land is fairly flat, never reaching higher than 8 feet (2.4 m) above sea level. The area contains a wide range of different species and habitats as a result of seasonal variations in water levels and the proportions of fresh and salt water. Because of its importance to wildlife, the southwestern part of the marsh, an area of 2,354 square miles (6,097 square km), has been made into a national park.

Six million years ago, all of the Everglades was submerged beneath a shallow sea. Since then, sea levels have dropped during ice ages and risen again between them. The Everglades area has been dry land when sea levels are low, and seabed when they are high.

RIVER OF GRASS

The modern Everglades have been described as a river of grass. In the natural cycle, water collects in Lake Okeechobee to the north of the marsh

between May and October. From there it flows southward over plains of sawgrass, then through mangrove swamps that border the Gulf of Mexico.

The water flows very slowly, moving around 100 feet (30 m) each day, but the river may be 50 miles (80 km) wide in places. The depth of water varies between 3 feet (0.9 m) in channels, or sloughs, and 6 inches (15 cm) elsewhere. A six-month dry season follows, and aquatic creatures must seek refuge in

▲ To preserve the wide range of habitats found in the Everglades, a large area of the marsh has been made into a national park.

▼ Small changes in elevation, levels of salt in the water, and soil types have a great effect on the types of plants, and hence animals, found in particular parts of the Everglades.

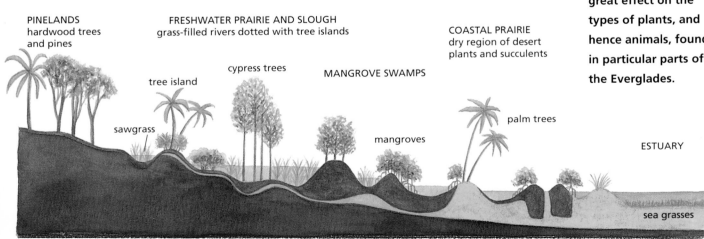

PINELANDS
hardwood trees and pines

FRESHWATER PRAIRIE AND SLOUGH
grass-filled rivers dotted with tree islands

COASTAL PRAIRIE
dry region of desert plants and succulents

cypress trees

MANGROVE SWAMPS

tree island

palm trees

sawgrass

mangroves

ESTUARY

sea grasses

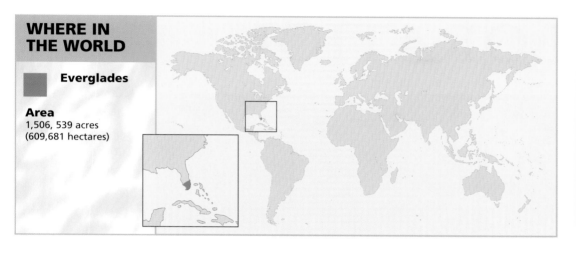

WHERE IN THE WORLD

Everglades

Area
1,506, 539 acres
(609,681 hectares)

SEE ALSO

- Alligator
- Eelgrass
- Estuary
- Gar
- Gulf of Mexico
- Manatee and dugong
- Mangrove swamp
- Nature preserve

the few deep pools that do not dry up. Fires often break out on the grasslands at this time, but they are beneficial to the Everglades, clearing away existing vegetation and making space for new growth.

DIVERSE ENVIRONMENT

There are many different habitats in the Everglades. Closest to the sea are shallow bays and estuaries, often carpeted with swaying sea grass. These places are home to many fish, shrimp, and mollusks in addition to rare species such as green turtles, crocodiles, and the Florida manatee. The bays are bordered by mangrove swamps, where red, black, and white mangroves flourish. Small fish and shrimp shelter among the mangrove roots, and many wading birds arrive during the dry season to feed, some even building their nests in the branches.

Freshwater habitats in the Everglades consist of the deep sloughs and, during the wet season, shallow, flooded prairies. Alligators, freshwater gars, largemouth bass, and killifish wait out the dry months in the sloughs, then spread out over the sawgrass plains to feed when the floods come.

Mosquitoes thrive during the wet season, and their larvae (young forms) are food for tiny mosquito fish.

The Everglades is a fragile habitat, and human activities threaten its existence. Today, water from Lake Okeechobee is diverted through a series of ditches and used for agriculture. This inevitably reduces the amount of water reaching the Everglades and increases the levels of pollution there.

Attempts to artificially control the water levels in the marsh have also harmed wildlife, since many of the native species have adapted to the seasonal rise and fall of the waters. ◆

▼ Sawgrass plants, such as this one, are widespread in the Everglades because they are able to withstand the natural cycle of dry and wet seasons.

EXPLORATION

FACT FILE

Alvin's career

1956
Allyn Vine of Woods Hole Oceanographic Institution attends conference where plans to design crewed undersea vehicles are made

1965
Alvin descends to 6,000 ft (1,800 m) on first crewed and untethered deep dive

1976
Alvin certified to depths of 13,000 ft (4,000 m)

1977
Crew discovers abundant animal life around hydrothermal vent in Pacific

1986
Discovery of new shrimp and an animal thought to be extinct at vent on midocean ridge. Visits wreck of *Titanic*

1990s
Vent explorations

Roughly 70 percent of Earth's surface is covered in water, yet our understanding of this vast area is limited. While almost all dry land has been charted and studied, scientists and explorers are only beginning to study the secrets of the ocean.

The most obvious reason for this delay is that humans are land animals, so they cannot reach many parts of the sea without the aid of sophisticated equipment. Much of this equipment has become available only in the last few decades. Perhaps of greatest significance has been the emergence of remote-sensing technologies, in which satellites map Earth's surface from space, allowing scientists to study the ocean from afar. Satellites, aircraft, research ships, and deep-diving submersibles all play a part in ocean exploration today.

A better knowledge of the ocean brings many benefits. Interactions between water and the atmosphere have profound effects on the climate. For example, the El Niño effect, which brings floods and droughts to many countries around the Pacific and beyond, is caused by a shift in the currents that circulate through that ocean. Understanding the interactions may help us to predict, and prepare for, this type of event.

The rocks and sediments on the seabed provide information about Earth's crust and the movements of the continents. They are also rich in valuable minerals and fossil fuels, such as oil and natural gas, which will become increasingly important as resources on land are exhausted. Seawater absorbs pollutants from the atmosphere and is home to a multitude of organisms. Since they release oxygen and absorb carbon dioxide, tiny plantlike algae (phyto-plankton) in the surface waters are vital in maintaining the planet's air quality.

RESEARCH PLATFORMS

The first ocean explorers relied on simple wooden sailing ships, but modern research vessels are often large and complex with an array of features to assist information gathering. Crews usually include a number of scientists from many different disciplines. Some study the chemistry and movements of seawater, while others collect samples of seabed rocks and sediments or investigate marine organisms. This allows a particular area to be explored in a variety of ways at the same time.

Research vessels may be fitted with bulky scientific equipment, such as drilling rigs for obtaining samples from beneath the seabed, or they may carry a number of smaller apparatus. Space is usually set aside for an onboard laboratory so that results can be analyzed during the voyage. A few of the most modern research ships use a twin-hull design. These craft provide greater deck space and are more stable than conventional single-hulled vessels. In addition, the sheltered area between the hulls can be used to deploy and recover scientific instruments and smaller craft.

Detailed study of the deep ocean has been made possible by submersibles. A submersible is basically any vessel designed to operate underwater, but the term is mostly used to describe the relatively small (compared to a submarine, for example) but well-equipped vessels used by scientists and explorers to study the ocean depths.

U.S.-designed *Alvin*, one of the first scientific submersibles to be built, has carried scientists to deep-sea hydrothermal vents, areas where new seabed is formed, and even to the wreck of the *Titanic*. *Alvin* is based around a thick metal sphere capable of withstanding enormous pressures at depths of up to 13,000 feet (4,000 m). Ballast tanks control its buoyancy, while thrusters give it great maneuverability underwater. Mechanical arms can be used to collect samples, which are placed in storage containers and transported back to the surface. The

▼ **Jacques Cousteau (1910–1997) was a French naval officer and marine explorer who made great advances in underwater exploration. In 1943, with Emile Gagnan, he developed the aqualung, an effective, self-contained underwater breathing apparatus for shallow diving.**

three-person crew—a pilot and two scientists—peer through a thick, cone-shaped window cut into the sphere. The craft is also fitted with video cameras and searchlights. Refitted several times, *Alvin* is over 35 years old and still in service. It has now been joined by a number of other submersibles. The Japanese-designed Shinkai 6500 is one that can operate to depths of up to 21,300 feet (6,500 m), or more than 4 miles (6.5 km) down, making it the deepest active submersible in the world.

Small remotely operated vehicles (ROVs) are useful for studying areas that are either inaccessible or too dangerous for a crewed submersible. Designed by scientists at the Woods Hole Oceanographic Institution, the autonomous benthic explorer (ABE) is a small cigar-shaped craft about 6 ft (2 m) long. It is used to explore and survey regions near the seafloor to depths of up to 18,000 ft (5,500 m).

NAVIGATION AT SEA

Accurate navigation is vital to ocean exploration. The ocean surface is largely devoid of landmarks that can be used for navigation, so past explorers used the positions of the stars as reference points to calculate their positions. However, this method is not very accurate, and readings can be taken only at certain times of day. A system called loran (*lo*ng-*ra*nge *n*avigation), introduced during World War II (1939–1945), improved the accuracy of navigation at sea. Loran consists of land-based transmitters that send out pulses of low-frequency radio waves. These pulses can be detected by ships thou-

▼ *Deep Rover* **leaving a semi-submersible barge. This one-person submersible has a strong but lightweight plastic sphere and thrusters that propel the craft in any direction.** *Deep Rover* **was recently used to look for giant squid in Kaikoura Canyon in the Pacific Ocean near New Zealand.**

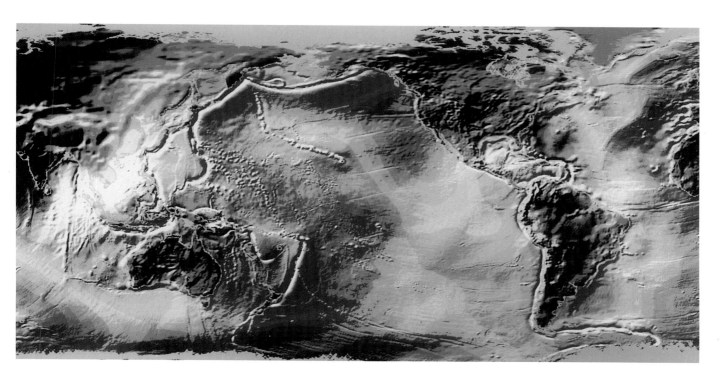

sands of miles away, and their precise timing can be used to determine position. Loran, too, has limitations. The transmitters are positioned to cover major shipping routes, and outside these areas the signals can become too weak to detect. A modern alternative called GPS (Global Positioning System) uses satellites orbiting Earth as transmitters, and it is accurate to within several feet anywhere in the world.

Satellites and aircraft are also used to study the oceans on a large scale. Radio waves, emitted from an aircraft in the high atmosphere or a satellite in space, travel through the air and bounce off the water surface. The time it takes for the waves to make the return journey can be used to calculate sea level. Variations in sea levels can indicate the presence of features such as underwater mountains and midocean ridges. Water temperature can also be detected from miles above the ocean, revealing the paths of surface currents. The color of the water

can be used to determine the concentration of living organisms, such as algae, which absorb red and blue light but reflect green.

Sonar is perhaps the most important technique for studying objects beneath the surface. Its principle is simple: an underwater transmitter sends out pulses of sound that travel through the water and reflect off any solid object they encounter. The echoes are detected by microphones, and their timing can be used to calculate water depth. Differences in depth reveal underwater objects or variations on the seabed.

Many methods are used to detect features beneath the seabed, such as oil and mineral deposits. One involves detonating explosives on or near the seafloor and measuring the resulting vibrations in underlying rocks. A more direct method is to drill a deep hole in the seabed and extract a core. Cores may be hundreds of feet long and contain samples from many layers of rocks. ◆

▲ This map of mean sea levels was made with data from a European Space Agency (ESA) satellite. The satellite carries an instrument that can accurately measure the distance between the satellite and the surface of Earth using radio waves. This technique can reveal underwater features.

SEE ALSO

- Archaeology
- Hydrothermal vent
- Oceanography
- Ocean trench
- Scuba diving and snorkeling

FIDDLER CRAB

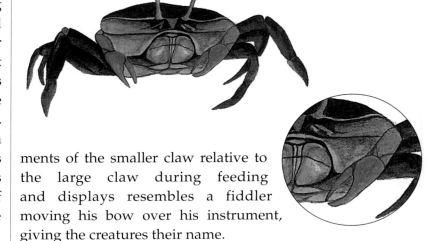

Many coastal mudflats, estuaries, and beaches throughout the warmer areas of the world, including the east and west coasts of the United States, contain populations of fiddler crabs. There are around 100 different species worldwide, and several types may inhabit a single beach. Adult male fiddler crabs are easily recognizable, because one of their claws is much bigger than the other. The larger claw is used in displays to threaten other males and to attract females. Both claws of females and young fiddler crabs are relatively small.

When the tide is out, fiddler crabs emerge from their burrows to feed on detritus (decaying plant and animal matter). They scoop up sand or mud, with their small claws in the case of the males, and sort it with specialized mouthparts. Food particles are eaten, while indigestible material is formed into little balls and spit out. The large claw is far too cumbersome for feeding, so mature males must work harder than females to get a meal. The move-ments of the smaller claw relative to the large claw during feeding and displays resembles a fiddler moving his bow over his instrument, giving the creatures their name.

USES OF THE BIGGER CLAW

Most fiddlers live in burrows that may extend up to 2 feet (60 cm) into the sand or mud. They dig using their smaller claws and legs. Male fiddler crabs are territorial, and they defend the space around the burrow from their neighbors and from wandering crabs. The burrow is important for the crabs, as it provides a place to shelter from predators (such as raccoons) and the Sun.

▲ Female fiddler crabs and the young of both sexes have two small claws, which they use to scoop sand or mud to the mouthparts when feeding.

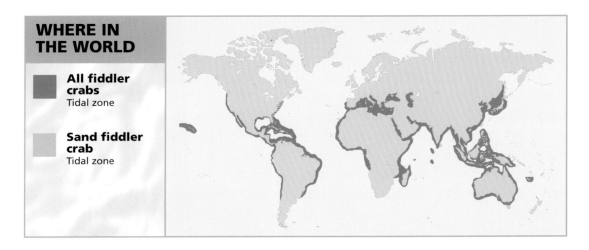

WHERE IN THE WORLD

■ **All fiddler crabs**
Tidal zone

■ **Sand fiddler crab**
Tidal zone

188

◄ A male fiddler crab living on a beach in western Africa signals by waving its large claw. This display may be to attract a mate or to deter a rival crab from wandering into its territory.

FACT FILE

Name
Sand fiddler crab (*Uca pugilator*)

Distinctive features
Adult males have one large claw

Habitat
Mud and sand flats along the east coast of North America

Food
Decaying particles of plant and animal matter

Breeding
Male displays large claw to attract a mate. Female carries eggs for up to 3 weeks, releasing them into the water after they have hatched

Lifespan
1–2 years

Size
½–1½ in (1–4 cm) across shell

The territory around the burrow is also protected for feeding and for attracting a mate. The male stands at the mouth of the burrow, waving the large claw; this acts as a threat to rival males. Fiddlers also make threatening sounds at rivals by rubbing their legs together and by rapping the ground or their shells with the large claw. Actual combat is rare in fiddlers, and despite the presence of the huge claw, injuries are uncommon. Encounters involve ritualized pushing and rubbing, often lasting for no more than a few seconds.

The large claw of the males is also used to attract a mate, and each species has its own unique display. The variation in displays prevents fiddlers of different species from attempting to breed, as females are only attracted to the displays of males of their own species. In some species, the male waves his large claw, extending it outward and upward before rapidly retracting it. Other types open and close their large claws or wave them up and down. Males may also flex their legs, bow, and drum the ground with their claws while displaying. The large claw is essential to the reproductive success of the males. Those that lose their large claws in combat or accidents are often mistaken for females.

Females usually seem indifferent to the male displays at first, but they are eventually attracted to one of the males, possibly the one displaying most energetically. Mating may take place inside the burrow but can also occur out in the open. Fiddler crabs are not easily distracted while mating, and they may stay together even when picked up.

◄ Although adult fiddlers dig their burrows above the waterline, they often make trips to the water's edge to moisten their gills and forage for food. Female fiddler crabs make trips underwater to release their hatched young.

THE LIFE OF THE FIDDLER CRAB

The female lays several thousand eggs, which she carries on the underside of her body until they hatch. The baby crabs, called larvae, begin their lives drifting in the ocean, feeding on plankton, and they look very different from the adults. In order to grow, crabs must molt their exoskeleton (the hard outer covering of the body). With each molt the larvae become increasingly crablike. Eventually, after five molts, the adults settle on a mudflat or beach and, after a period of wandering, find a spot to dig their burrows. Of the thousands of eggs produced by each female, only a few survive to adulthood. Many larvae are never swept back to land, and a large number are eaten by predators.

Fiddler crabs need to stay close to water, since they must keep their gills moist in order to breathe. At low tide, fiddlers can get water from within their burrow, and they can also absorb water through tufts of hair on their legs.

Fiddlers are still relatively common, and they are not commercially gathered. However, their habitats are decreasing with coastal development and are often damaged by pollution. ◆

SEE ALSO
- Crab
- Crustacean
- Estuary
- Invertebrate
- Mangrove swamp